Leadership and Influence

Independent Study 240.a

May 2010

 FEMA

TABLE OF CONTENTS

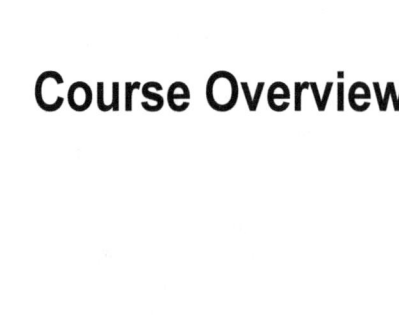

Course Overview

About This Course

Being able to lead others—to motivate them to commit their energies and expertise to achieving the shared mission and goals of the emergency management system—is a necessary and vital part of every emergency manager, planner, and responder's job. This course is designed to improve your leadership and influence skills. It addresses:

- Leadership from within.

- How to facilitate change.

- How to build and rebuild trust.

- Using personal influence and political savvy.

- Fostering an environment for leadership development.

FEMA's Independent Study Program

The Federal Emergency Management Agency's (FEMA's) Independent Study Program is one of the delivery channels that the Emergency Management Institute (EMI) uses to provide training to the general public and specific audiences. This course is part of FEMA's Independent Study Program. In addition to this course, the Independent Study Program includes courses in floodplain management, radiological emergency management, the role of the emergency manager, hazardous materials, disaster assistance, the role of the Emergency Operations Center, and an orientation to community disaster exercises.

FEMA's independent study courses are available at no charge and include a final examination. You may apply individually or through group enrollment. When enrolling for a course, you must include your name, mailing address, social security number, and the title of the course that you want to enroll in.

FEMA's Independent Study Program (Continued)

If you need assistance with enrollment, or if you have questions about how to enroll, contact the Independent Study Program at:

FEMA Independent Study Program
Administrative Office
Emergency Management Institute
16825 South Seton Avenue
Emmitsburg, MD 21727
(301) 447-1200

Information about FEMA's Independent Study Program also is available on the Internet at:

http://training.fema.gov/IS/

Each request will be reviewed and directed to the appropriate course manager or program office for assistance.

Final Examination

This course includes a written final examination, which you must complete and return to FEMA's Independent Study Office for scoring. To obtain credit for taking this course, you must successfully complete (75% correct) this examination regardless of whether you complete this course through self-instruction or through group instruction.

You may take the final examination as many times as necessary.

Course Completion

The course completion deadline for all FEMA Independent Study courses is 1 year from the date of enrollment. The date of enrollment is the date that the EMI Independent Study Office will use for completion of all required course work, including the final examination. If you do not complete this course, including the final examination, within that timeframe, your enrollment will be terminated.

Leadership and Influence has no prerequisites. However, it is recommended that you complete the other courses in the Professional Development Series—*Effective Communication* and *Decision Making and Problem Solving*—before taking this course.

How to Complete This Course

Work through this course at a pace that is comfortable for you. You should resist the temptation to rush through the material, however. Take enough time with each unit to ensure that you have mastered its content before proceeding to the next.

Knowledge Checks

To help you know when to proceed, each unit is followed by a Knowledge Check that addresses the material contained in the unit. The Knowledge Check asks you to answer questions that apply to what you have learned in the unit. The answers to the Knowledge Check follow each Knowledge Check.

When you finish each exercise, check your answers, and review the parts of the text that you do not understand. Do not proceed to the next unit until you are sure that you have mastered the current unit.

When you have completed all of the units, complete the final exam online, or use the answer sheet (if provided in your course packet). EMI will score your test and notify you of the results.

Begin the Course

You may begin the course now.

Unit 1: Course Introduction

Introduction

As an emergency management professional, you must be able to use leadership and influence effectively to lead your organization and the community in planning for, preventing, and responding to emergency situations and disasters. Leadership involves providing vision, direction, coordination, and motivation toward achieving emergency management goals. These skills are necessary whether dealing with subordinates, those with more authority than you, your peers in partner organizations, volunteers, or the public.

Unit 1 Objectives

After completing this unit, you should be able to:

- Review the main topics that will be covered in this course.

- Relate the topics to your job and community.

- Determine a strategy for completing the course successfully.

Leadership in Emergency Management: What's at Stake?

It probably goes without saying that leadership is critically important when emergencies happen. By its very nature, emergency management connotes leadership—safeguarding life and property by marshalling both the will and the required resources to respond to and recover from an emergency quickly.

To illustrate what can happen when emergency personnel cannot or do not exercise effective leadership, read the following case study and answer the accompanying questions.

Case Study 1.1: The Los Cuchillos Fire

The Los Cuchillos Fire started as a result of a private aircraft crash in the rugged Los Cuchillos Hills area. Local firefighters responded at 8:00 a.m. By noon, as the fire quickly grew to 20,000 acres in scrub brushland, the Los Cuchillos Fire Department invoked its mutual aid agreements. This bolstered the firefighting force by two teams. Even with five wildland fire strike teams on the fire, the fire had spread to 40,000 acres by 6:00 p.m.

At 6:15 p.m., with all department and mutual aid fire assets committed, Fire Chief Ed Blakely called the County Emergency Operations Center (EOC) and requested that Emergency Manager Fran Tinsley ask for outside help. Mrs. Tinsley phoned the duty officer at the State EOC, Ellen Burgess. Mrs. Tinsley requested that the State Emergency Response Act be invoked. Under the Emergency Response Act, the State Director of Emergency Management could commit State assets (people, equipment, and money) to the fire.

Ellen Burgess contacted Chief Blakely in the field. He quickly communicated the situation: "This fire is taking off and I cannot hold it. I have got three of my strike teams committed and two mutual aid teams on site. The well has run dry. Not only that, but this fire is headed straight for the Tres Rios Nuclear Power Plant. In fact, it just crossed the plant boundary and is only a mile-and-a-half from the plant itself. It is also threatening the Los Cerros housing community. You need to invoke the Emergency Response Act because I am going to need State resources."

The State EOC had already been activated to monitor the situation as Acting State Director Rick Douglas considered the County's request for State help. Rick was a cautious decisionmaker. He had encountered problems in the past when he had made decisions without getting all of the facts. Ellen Burgess stated, "The fire is out of control, mutual aid assets are committed, and the fire is headed for a nuclear power plant. There is really not much to think about."

Case Study 1.1: The Los Cuchillos Fire (Continued)

Rick and Ellen did not work well together. Each felt that the other was untrustworthy and, as a result, there was little cooperation or communication between them. Rick turned his back on Ellen and pondered the request. The pace of State operations quickened as media calls came in requesting information on the fire. EOC staff were busy fielding the media calls, drafting situation reports, and trying to plot the location and size of the fire.

Ellen confronted Rick with some issues. "Look, we need to move out on this thing. What is there to decide? The fire is out of control and heading for the nuclear power plant. They are overwhelmed even with mutual aid. We need to decide now, and we need to activate our full emergency staff here with an increased staffing pattern and shift schedule for the EOC."

Rick backed away, holding his head and said, "Enough! You are making my head hurt. I am not going to make any kind of decision until I know how many fire rigs are on the scene." He then directed the Operations Section Chief to call the fire scene to find out how many fire assets were committed. This took several minutes and did not produce a satisfactory answer when Chief Blakely confessed that he was not exactly sure how many rigs were on the scene because the two mutual aid teams had not reported their strength.

At 6:50 p.m., County Commissioner Vera Morgan called the EOC. Ellen fielded the call, called Rick over, and put Vera on the speakerphone.

"We have just lost two homes in the Los Cerros community, and I want something done immediately, Rick. Invoke the Emergency Resource Act now!"

"I am working on it right now, Commissioner," Rick replied. "I will get right back to you."

As he hung up, Ellen noted, "She is one upset lady. We have got to invoke the Emergency Response Act. Those people need help now!"

"Okay, okay, don't push me."

Finally, at 7:20 p.m., after Operations learned from Chief Blakely that seven houses in the Los Cerros area were destroyed and that the fire had spread to within a half mile of the nuclear power plant, Rick invoked the Emergency Response Act and released State firefighting assets from nearby Mancos State Park to deploy to the fire.

By the time the fire was controlled, it had grown to 65,000 acres, destroyed seven homes and two businesses, and burned within 300 yards of the nuclear plant. The State response time would be an issue in the Los Cuchillos community.

Case Study 1.1: The Los Cuchillos Fire (Continued)

Questions:

- What leadership problems do you see at the EOC?

- What are the likely consequences of the leadership problems?

Case Study 1.1: The Los Cuchillos Fire (Continued)

Answers to Case Study

What leadership problems do you see at the EOC?

Rick has not created an environment in the EOC that is conducive to effective leadership. He neither seeks nor accepts input to decisions that are clearly difficult for him, and he appears to be paralyzed by his own political agendas, the pressure to decide quickly, and a self-preservation mentality.

Ellen is a party to the climate of distrust that pervades the EOC. Neither she nor Rick appears to have worked at building a trusting relationship, and each contributes to the communication barriers. Although Ellen's analysis of the emergency situation appears right, and she attempts to persuade Rick to see her view of the situation, she presents her input in a way that ignores Rick's perspective and puts him on the defensive.

What are the probable consequences of the leadership problem?

Rick's inability to respond quickly results in delays and loss of property. The consequences to human safety could have been much worse if the fire had reached the nuclear plant. There will undoubtedly be a loss of trust within the community as well as within the emergency management network.

Leadership and Influence in Emergency Management

As the case study illustrates, leadership is critically important in emergency management, and lack of it can result in loss of public trust, loss of property, or worse.

And the need for leadership and influence is not confined to the response and recovery phases of emergency management. Effective leadership is equally necessary for implementing mitigation programs and for emergency management preparedness and disaster prevention.

In all of these phases of emergency management, leadership and influence can take many forms. For example, you are leading and influencing when you:

- Invite other members of an emergency management team to a meeting to discuss common goals.

- Use that meeting as an opportunity to really listen, to learn "where they're coming from" and what they're aiming for.

- Ask for help with or input on a project that will help your community prepare for disasters.

- Speak out to persuade others to accept your point of view.

- Encourage someone else to assume the leadership role in a group.

- Work to establish partnerships with neighboring communities to share resources for prevention, preparedness, response, recovery, or mitigation.

- Recognize the differences among people and drawing on the strengths of your organization to prepare for emergencies.

- Marshal local resources to respond during an emergency.

- Demonstrate high standards of honesty, integrity, trust, openness, and respect for others.

These are only a few examples. You can probably think of many other leadership roles that you or those around you fulfill in the day-to-day operations of your job.

Mandates: Incident Management and Coordination Systems

On February 28, 2003, the President issued Homeland Security Presidential Directive 5 (HSPD–5), "Management of Domestic Incidents," which directed the Secretary of Homeland Security to develop and administer a National Incident Management System (NIMS). This system provides a consistent nationwide template to enable Federal, State, tribal, and local governments, nongovernmental organizations (NGOs), and the private sector to work together to prevent, protect against, respond to, recover from, and mitigate the effects of incidents, regardless of cause, size, location, or complexity. This consistency provides the foundation for utilization of NIMS for all incidents, ranging from daily occurrences to incidents requiring a coordinated Federal response.

National Incident Management System (NIMS)

NIMS is not an operational incident management or resource allocation plan. NIMS represents a core set of doctrines, concepts, principles, terminology, and organizational processes that enables effective, efficient, and collaborative incident management.

Building on the foundation provided by existing emergency management and incident response systems used by jurisdictions, organizations, and functional disciplines at all levels, NIMS integrates best practices into a comprehensive framework for use nationwide by emergency management/response personnel in an all-hazards context. These best practices lay the groundwork for the components of NIMS and provide the mechanisms for the further development and refinement of supporting national standards, guidelines, protocols, systems, and technologies. NIMS fosters the development of specialized technologies that facilitate emergency management and incident response activities, and allows for the adoption of new approaches that will enable continuous refinement of the system over time.

NIMS (Continued)

Five major components make up the NIMS system approach:

- **Preparedness:** Effective emergency management and incident response activities begin with a host of preparedness activities conducted on an ongoing basis, in advance of any potential incident. Preparedness involves an integrated combination of assessment; planning; procedures and protocols; training and exercises; personnel qualifications, licensure, and certification; equipment certification; and evaluation and revision.

- **Communications and Information Management:** Emergency management and incident response activities rely on communications and information systems that provide a common operating picture to all command and coordination sites. NIMS describes the requirements necessary for a standardized framework for communications and emphasizes the need for a common operating picture. This component is based on the concepts of interoperability, reliability, scalability, and portability, as well as the resiliency and redundancy of communications and information systems.

- **Resource Management:** Resources (such as personnel, equipment, or supplies) are needed to support critical incident objectives. The flow of resources must be fluid and adaptable to the requirements of the incident. NIMS defines standardized mechanisms and establishes the resource management process to identify requirements, order and acquire, mobilize, track and report, recover and demobilize, reimburse, and inventory resources.

- **Command and Management:** The Command and Management component of NIMS is designed to enable effective and efficient incident management and coordination by providing a flexible, standardized incident management structure. The structure is based on three key organizational constructs: the Incident Command System, Multiagency Coordination Systems, and Public Information.

- **Ongoing Management and Maintenance:** Within the auspices of Ongoing Management and Maintenance, there are two components: the National Integration Center (NIC) and Supporting Technologies.

Additional information about NIMS can be accessed online at http://www.fema.gov/emergency/nims/ or by completing EMI's IS 700 online course.

National Response Framework (NRF)

The NRF is a guide to how the Nation conducts all-hazards response – from the smallest incident to the largest catastrophe. This key document establishes a comprehensive, national, all-hazards approach to domestic incident response. The Framework identifies the key response principles, roles, and structures that organize national response. It describes how communities, States, the Federal Government, and private-sector and nongovernmental partners apply these principles for a coordinated, effective national response.

The NRF is:

- **Always in effect, and elements can be implemented as needed on a flexible, scalable basis to improve response.** It is not always obvious at the outset whether a seemingly minor event might be the initial phase of a larger, rapidly growing threat. The NRF allows for the rapid acceleration of response efforts without the need for a formal trigger mechanism.

- **Part of a broader strategy.** The NRF is required by, and integrates under, a larger National Strategy for Homeland Security that:
  - Serves to guide, organize, and unify our Nation's homeland security efforts.

  - Reflects our increased understanding of the threats confronting the United States.

  - Incorporates lessons learned from exercises and real-world catastrophes.

  - Articulates how we should ensure our long-term success by strengthening the homeland security foundation we have built.

- **Comprised of more than the core document.** The NRF is comprised of the core document, the Emergency Support Function (ESF), Support, and Incident Annexes, and the Partner Guides. The core document describes the doctrine that guides our national response, roles and responsibilities, response actions, response organizations, and planning requirements to achieve an effective national response to any incident that occurs.

  The following documents provide more detailed information to assist practitioners in implementing the Framework:

  - **Emergency Support Function Annexes** group Federal resources and capabilities into functional areas that are most frequently needed in a national response (e.g., Transportation, Firefighting, Search and Rescue).

NRF (Continued)

- **Support Annexes** describe essential supporting aspects that are common to all incidents (e.g., Financial Management, Volunteer and Donations Management, Private-Sector Coordination).

- **Incident Annexes** address the unique aspects of how we respond to seven broad incident categories (e.g., Biological, Nuclear/Radiological, Cyber, Mass Evacuation).

Additional information about the NRF can be accessed online at http://www.fema.gov/emergency/NRF/ or by completing EMI's IS 800.b online course.

What This Means to You

Your jurisdiction is required to:

- Use NIMS to manage all incidents, including recurring and/or planned special events.

- Integrate all response agencies and entities into a single, seamless system, from the Incident Command Post, through department Emergency Operations Centers (DEOCs) and local Emergency Operations Centers (EOCs), through the State EOC to the regional- and national-level entities.

- Develop and implement a public information system.

- Identify and type all resources according to established standards.

- Ensure that all personnel are trained properly for the job(s) they perform.

- Ensure communications interoperability and redundancy.

Remember the importance of working with VOADs, NGOs, business and industry, and others to develop a plan for addressing volunteer needs *before* an emergency to help eliminate some of the potential problems that can occur *during* an emergency.

Leadership and Influence: What Do They Mean?

So, exactly what do we mean by leadership? How does it differ (if at all) from management? And where does influence fit in?

Organizational development literature contains a wide range of definitions and descriptions of leadership. Some people argue that leadership and management are quite different and that they require different perspectives and skills. Others hold the view that leadership is a facet of management and that influencing is a facet of leadership.

In the context of this course, we'll take the broad view:

> **A leader is someone who sets direction and influences people to follow that direction.**

By this definition, a manager may or may not be a leader. This course is about developing the skills that are needed to become an effective leader.

Leadership theories. There are numerous theories about leadership and about carrying out the role of the leader. Although this course will not delve into these theories in any depth, you may wish to seek more information on your own. Some of these theories include:

- Servant leader.

- Democratic leader.

- Principle-centered leader.

- Group-man theory.

- Great-man theory.

- Traits theory.

- Visionary leader.

- Total leader.

- Situational leader.

Leadership and Influence: What Do They Mean? (Continued)

Leadership styles. Leaders carry out their roles in a wide variety of styles. Leadership style is influenced by the individual's beliefs, values, and assumptions, as well as the organizational culture and the situation. Styles that have been identified include autocratic, laissez-faire, democratic, and others.

Again, we will not study particular styles in any detail in this course, but you may wish to research these styles on your own.

Course Objectives

This course is designed to promote effective leadership and influencing skills among emergency management personnel. At the conclusion of this course, you should be able to:

- Explain what leadership means for emergency personnel.

- Explain why effective leadership begins with personal insight and development.

- Identify your leadership capabilities and areas for personal development.

- Describe a change management model for emergency management and the process for planning, communicating, and implementing change.

- Describe how to build and rebuild trust in an organization.

- Use personal influence and develop political savvy to network and influence people effectively.

- Develop strategies for creating a positive work environment that fosters leadership and a commitment to continuous improvement in others.

Course Content

This course is composed of seven units.

- **Unit 1** offers an overview of the course content.

- **Unit 2** discusses what it means to be self-aware and the link between self-awareness and leadership.

- **Unit 3** explores the topic of change and how to facilitate change effectively in the work environment.

- **Unit 4** focuses on the importance of building trust as a foundation for effective leadership and change management and examines strategies for building and rebuilding trust.

- **Unit 5** addresses personal influence and political savvy and their role in each phase of emergency management.

- **Unit 6** examines the critical elements of a leadership environment and presents strategies for fostering such an environment.

- **Unit 7** summarizes the course content. At the conclusion of Unit 7, you will have an opportunity to evaluate your success in meeting your personal course goals.

Activity: Self-Assessment: Leadership Behaviors

The purpose of this activity is to assess your leadership skills and priorities.

Instructions:

1. Fill out the questionnaire on the following page, as follows.

    Imagine that you have a finite amount of time and skill with which to lead your department or work group (which, by the way, you do).

    *   In **column one**, assess your current proficiency in the 15 leadership behaviors by rating yourself on a percentage basis (0% – 100%) for each behavior.
    *   In **column two**, estimate how much time you spend on the 15 behaviors by apportioning your sum total (100%) of actual time spent among the roles.
    *   In **column three**, assess where you **need** to be spending your time for your work group to excel. Again, apportion your sum total (100%) of where you should be spending your time among the 15 tasks.

    Each column must total 100%, but not every individual item may have a number in it. If other words, if you feel you have no skill in an area, or devote no time to it, you will leave that box blank.

2. After you have filled out the questionnaire, complete the questions that follow.

Activity: Self-Assessment: Leadership Behaviors (Continued)

Leadership Behaviors	How proficient are you in this behavior?	How much time do you spend on this behavior?	For your group to excel, how <u>should</u> you apportion your time?
1. Plan for the future			
2. Remain up to date with emerging issues and trends			
3. Communicate a sense of where the organization will be over the long term			
4. Foster commitment			
5. Emphasize organizational values			
6. Challenge people with new goals and aspirations			
7. Create a sense of excitement or urgency			
8. Inspire people to take action			
9. Manage the efficiency of operations			
10. Evaluate proposed projects			
11. Integrate conflicting perspectives and needs			
12. Manage performance			
13. Focus on results			
14. Solve problems			
15. Influence operational decisions			
TOTALS	N/A	100%	100%

Adapted from *Deep Change* by Quinn, Robert E. Jossey-Bass: San Francisco, 1996 (p. 149).

Activity: Personal Learning Goals

Based on the self-assessment that you have just completed, the content outlined for this course, and the course objectives, identify two or three specific learning goals for yourself. Write your goals in the space below, and use them as a reference for the course.

Personal Goals

1.

2.

3.

Summary and Transition

Unit 1 provided an overview of the course content and asked you to identify personal leadership goals. Unit 2 discusses how self-knowledge and understanding contribute to effective leadership.

For More Information

FEMA EMI Independent Study Course IS-700: *National Incident Management System (NIMS), An Introduction*

National Incident Management System (NIMS):
www.fema.gov/emegency/NIMS

National Response Framework (NRF):
http://www.fema.gov/emergency/nrf

Unit 2: Leadership from Within

Introduction

This unit focuses on leadership from within—the relationship between self-knowledge and effective leadership. Part of being an effective leader is the ability to create an environment that encourages self-discovery and the testing of assumptions that may impede growth, change, and the development of a shared vision. As we work to increase self-knowledge, balance inquiry and advocacy, and solicit authentic feedback, we free ourselves—and our organization—to embrace constructive change.

Unit 2 Objectives

After completing this unit, you should be able to:

- Describe how self-knowledge and understanding contribute to effective leadership.

- Use self-assessment, self-reflection, and authentic feedback to increase your self-knowledge.

- Identify factors that underlie your thought process and affect your ability to lead.

- Differentiate inquiry and advocacy and identify strategies for balancing the two.

- Identify personal goals for improving your inner capacity for leadership.

Where Leadership Begins

In his book, *Leading from the Inside Out*, Kevin Cashman said:

> "We tend to view leadership as an external event . . . as something
> we do. Rather, leadership is an intimate expression of who we are;
> it is our being in action."

In other words, we tend to think of leadership as telling others what to do
instead of looking inside ourselves and thinking about how our leadership
actions reflect who we are. Thus, instead of thinking, "What action should I take
in this situation?" perhaps we ought to think more broadly and look at how our
view of the world impacts our decisions, and how the messages that we send
through our language and actions impact others.

Paradigms that Guide Thinking

The word *paradigm* tends to be overused, and it is often thought of as a
"leftover" from the 1990s. Nonetheless, paradigms help us understand why
people have different views of reality.

Paradigms are mental models that provide a structure for our thoughts and
guide our thinking. They help us make sense of all of the information that we
encounter by telling us what to pay attention to, how to arrange what we pay
attention to, how to draw conclusions, and how to interpret things. This process
is guided by a set of unconscious assumptions that we carry to make sense of
what we experience.

We develop our paradigms over time from our family, region of the country,
cultural niche, organizations—any environment in which we learn the written or
unwritten rules that guide our behavior.

Paradigms are useful in that they help us structure how to think about and act in
a situation. They cause problems when we think that **our** paradigm is the **only**
paradigm. When we view people who have different paradigms as thinking in
confusing, unpredictable, irrational, immoral, or unethical ways, it frequently
creates conflict.

Three Work Paradigms

We think of ourselves in many different ways at work. Sometimes we are focused on our work or the work of our immediate group. Sometimes we are trying to "get along" with others, and keeping things working as best as they can. Sometimes we have a broader vision of our place in our organization and our influence over it.

We can see these as three common work paradigms, and understand how each impacts our work and that or our entire organization. We will refer to the paradigms we will discuss as:

- The Hired Hand

- The Broker

- The Leader

We don't work out of just one of these paradigms at a given time and for any given situation. They complement each other, and we draw upon them based on our reaction to the situation at hand, and in order to address it.

The chart on the next page provides an overview of how operating out of each of these paradigms causes us to view and react to different aspects of our work. Those differences are then described on the following pages.

Three Work Paradigms (Continued)

Three Work Paradigms			
	The Hired Hand	The Broker	The Leader
Sees Organization As...	A means of facilitating their work	A system of mutual interests that help each other to achieve individual goals	People working together to achieve a greater goal
Source of Power...	Competence or perceived competence	Ability to manage interactions between units	Others trust in them
Perceives Senior Management As...	Bureaucratic, obstacle to progress	Granter of rights and privileges	Means of providing vision, direction
Handles Opposition By...	Making logical, fact-based arguments	Making compromises to get what they want	Listening to others, advocating their own position
Communication Style...	Stick to the facts	Tries to make sense of the facts	Understanding and being understood
Main Goal...	Advancing their work	Improving their position in the hierarchy	Define a vision and work toward achieving it

Sees the Organization as...

The Hired Hand sees the organization as a means to an end. They want to accomplish their work and need the organization to facilitate it. The barometers of the success of the organization, its units and its employees is whether or not each completes the work they set out to do, and how well they do it.

The Broker wants to accomplish their goals as well, but sees the organization as made up of smaller groups of individuals working together to achieve their own goals. They judge the organization on how well its units and individuals interact and "cut deals" to get work done.

The Leader sees the organization as made up of individuals working together to set and meet goals they couldn't achieve by themselves. The ability to work effectively together, to make the sum greater than its parts, is the standard to judge the organization by.

Source of Power...

The Hired Hand gets credibility from their ability to be the best at their job. Their power is based on both their technical competence and from how others view their competence (their reputation).

The Broker's credibility stems from their position within the hierarchy of the organization. The Brokers who get things done are the most successful.

The Leader's credibility is based in their integrity and others' belief in it. Their greatest asset is others' trust in them. They wield their power to empower others.

Perceives Senior Management As...

The Hired Hand feels that in a perfect world, there would be no need for senior management. It produces nothing and gets in the way of progress.

The Broker perceives senior management as a grantor of privileges and people to curry favor from. Being a member of senior management is a great honor since it allows them to make decisions that impact many.

The Leader understands that senior management is there to lead and provide vision. Senior management should set the proper moral tone for the organization and "do the right thing".

Handles Opposition By...

The Hired Hand will engage in argument based on empirical evidence and fact. They appeal to the rational in those that oppose them.

The Broker works out of the "I'll scratch your back if you scratch mine" school of conflict management. Compromises are made that provide what they, and whoever they are making deals with, to get what they want.

The Leader strives to fairly address complex and competing needs in any situation, and thinks of creative, equitable solutions to any challenge.

Communication Style...

The Hired Hand sticks to the facts – everything else is nonsense that distracts people from the true issue at hand.

The Broker focuses on the facts but tries to make sense of them, ascribing meaning to create a big picture of what discrete events mean when considered together.

The Leader realizes that humans look for meaning beyond the simple facts, and is sensitive to the perceived meaning of their actions. They strive to understand others as well as be understood.

Main Goal...

The Hired Hand wants to advance their own work and receive credit for it.

The Broker wants to advance their work as well, but in this case it is their position within the hierarchy.

The Leader is focused on defining and carrying out goals for the common good.

Activity: Which Paradigm?

Instructions: Read the following descriptions of how different people approach their leadership roles. Decide which leadership paradigm each one represents:

A. **The Hired Hand**
B. **The Broker**
C. **The Leader**

You may mark more than one box if appropriate.

	A	B	C
1. Jane is working toward an alliance with the smaller neighboring jurisdictions because she's convinced that a comprehensive, cooperative response capability will best serve the citizenry.	☐	☐	☐
2. Buck's rank and seniority carry a lot of weight with his employees. He's the boss, he knows the ropes, and he works hard. So they do too.	☐	☐	☐
3. Corina wants to get the Emergency Operations Plan (EOP) revised quickly and according to the current guidelines because Regional will be reviewing the plan next month.	☐	☐	☐
4. Robert is convinced that the new Standard Operating Procedures (SOPs) just create a lot of busywork. No one at Headquarters has enough field experience to understand what really goes on.	☐	☐	☐
5. The consensus among Jim's employees and colleagues is that he is someone you can count on to be fair, principled, and beyond reproach. The new strategic plan seems a little scary to some, because it means a lot of changes, but he hasn't let them down in the past.	☐	☐	☐
6. Anna has locked horns with other response agencies over equipment resources. She decides to give in on the staffing issue to get access to the needed debris removal equipment.	☐	☐	☐

Activity: Which Paradigm? (Continued)

Check your answers against the following:

	A	B	C
1. Jane is working toward an alliance with the smaller neighboring jurisdictions because she is convinced that a comprehensive, cooperative response capability will best serve the citizenry. **The Leader's main goal is to define and carry out a vision for the common good.**	☐	☐	☑
2. Buck's rank and seniority carry a lot of weight with his employees. He is the boss, he knows the ropes, and he works hard. So they do too. **The Broker derives credibility and power from their rank within the hierarchy.**	☐	☑	☐
3. Corina wants to get the Emergency Operations Plan (EOP) revised quickly and according to the current guidelines because Regional will be reviewing the plan next month. **Both Individual Contributors and Managers have advancing their own work as their main goal.**	☑	☑	☐
4. Robert is convinced that the new Standard Operating Procedures (SOPs) just create a lot of busywork. No one at Headquarters has enough field experience to understand what really goes on. **The Hired Hand sees senior management as an obstacle to progress.**	☑	☐	☐
5. The consensus among Jim's employees and colleagues is that he is someone you can count on to be fair, principled, and beyond reproach. The new strategic plan seems a little scary to some, because it means a lot of changes, but he has not let them down in the past. **The Leader's credibility is based in their integrity and others' belief in it. Their greatest asset is others' trust in them.**	☐	☐	☑
6. Anna has locked horns with other response agencies over equipment resources. She decides to give in on the staffing issue to get access to the needed debris removal equipment. **The Broker's approach to opposition tends to be compromise—making deals to get what they and whoever they are making deals with to get what they want.**	☐	☑	☐

Balancing the Paradigms

Three Lenses of Leadership

We have examined three different ways of looking at the world. Is one right and are the others wrong? Of course not. Everyone displays attributes of all three. However, we can see that those acting out of the paradigm of the Leader will be most effective and have the greatest impact over time.

In the final analysis, your paradigm is a way of thinking that guides your behavior, decisions, and actions. Given the complexity of the challenges you encounter as an emergency management professional today and in the future, you'll want your thinking to be as multidimensional as possible.

The three paradigms will help you expand the range of your thinking. Think of them as three lenses through which to view a situation and determine your actions.

Three Lenses of Leadership (Continued)

Telescopic lens. The telescopic lens has the longest term view. When you look through this lens, you're more likely to:

- Establish your beliefs and values and be consistent with them.

- Determine a course for change in the future and articulate it as a vision.

- Stimulate coworkers and yourself to challenge traditional ways of thinking.

- Develop yourself and others to the highest levels of potential.

Mid-distance lens. When you look through the mid-distance lens, your view is focused on short term goals. You're likely to focus on articulating standards, expectations, goals, and rewards, and the consequences for not meeting expectations.

Microscopic lens. When you look through the microscopic lens, your view is like that of the individual contributor. You may be part of a task force or team where your focus is on detail-oriented, task-specific work and your style is more laid back.

For most of us, growing as a leader requires us to become aware of our paradigms and develop the ability to view situations through the three lenses just described.

What it takes. To do this, you may need to let go of behaviors and beliefs about leadership that are comfortable for you but that no longer serve you well. You may have to stop doing some things you're good at and love to do, and instead delegate them to someone else to further that person's professional development. Or, you may begin to rethink behaviors that haven't served you well and consider how to change them.

Benefits. Moving away from old habits and out of your comfort zone can free you to expand the ways in which you think about leadership, change your behaviors and actions to become more effective, and move freely between the paradigms through more conscious choices.

The Case for Self-Knowledge

The first step in this process of leadership growth is developing self-knowledge. Self-knowledge is an awareness of our internal feelings, preferences, biases, strengths, and weaknesses.

What are some of the ways that increased self-knowledge can strengthen you as a leader? Take a few moments to jot your ideas in the space below.

Self-knowledge can make me a stronger leader in the following ways:

Benefits of Increased Self-Knowledge

Self-knowledge is a common trait among great leaders. Effective leaders tend to look inside themselves. They are centered, have an internal locus of control, and exhibit self-understanding and self-confidence. Most leaders find that increased self-knowledge helps them:

- Understand others.

- Understand and manage their reactions to others.

- Appreciate others' points of view.

- Leverage their strengths.

- Strengthen or compensate for their weaknesses.

- Earn trust.

- Be aware of how they impact others, both positively and negatively.

- Have more self-confidence.

The Johari Window

The Johari Window, shown below, is a model that gives us a visual way to think about self-knowledge.

JOHARI WINDOW

	Known to Self	Unknown to Self
Known to Others	Open Area	Blind Area
Unknown to Others	Hidden Area	Unknown Area

Joe Luft and Harry Ingham

This model delineates four quadrants involved in interpersonal relationships:

- The **open area** is what we both know about me and openly share.

- The **hidden area** is what I hide from you about myself.

- The **blind area** is what you know about me—what you keep from me, what you observe about me, or think or feel about me, of which I am unaware.

- The **unknown area** is part of me, from my past, about which neither one of us yet knows, at least on a conscious level.

Expanding the Open Area

The more we can increase the parts of ourselves that are known to self and others, the greater our potential for building effective relationships, both at home and in the workplace.

Benefits. You've already considered some of the benefits of increasing the area that you know about yourself. But increasing what *others* know about you is one of the most important things you can do to build trust with those you lead.

When leaders make their reasoning and thinking apparent to others, they build trust over time. As a result, others are then more willing to give them the benefit of the doubt during those times when the leader can't share information.

Opening Up. Becoming more open means showing people more of your thinking, more of the things that you are wrestling with, more about your objectives, and your likes and dislikes with respect to the "business" of emergency management. It means making yourself more *available*. (Remember, though, we're talking about work-related issues, not personal issues.)

Expanding the Open Area (Continued)

Test for yourself to see if this is true: have the leaders you really trusted and respected been more open about themselves than other leaders? Did they let you in on their preferences, biases, strengths, and weaknesses with respect to work issues?

True—being more open involves some risk. But the potential payoff is greater trust, understanding, and the benefit of the doubt when it's needed.

Ways to Increase Self-Knowledge

Whether or not you consider yourself a self-aware person, there are many ways to learn more about yourself and how you lead. Three important methods include:

- Self-assessment.

- Self-reflection.

- Soliciting authentic feedback.

Self-Assessment

We tend to be an outward-oriented society. That tendency leads us to think that both our problems and their solutions are outside of us. Our culture doesn't put a high priority on self-assessment.

Significance. The upside of this is that we become good at recognizing and analyzing the world outside ourselves. But the downside is that we tend to overlook the ways in which we ourselves are impacting the world around us. We tend to be less aware of the choices we make, our own responses to situations, and our own resources that can help us succeed.

Our outward orientation can blind us to perhaps our most important and readily available resources: our own talents, preferences, and choices.

Self-Assessment (Continued)

Approaches. In the previous unit, you completed a simple self-assessment that focused on proficiency and time spent on various leadership activities. You can repeat that assessment from time to time to maintain awareness of your leadership skills and growth. Job Aid 2.1 on pages 2.35 and 2.36 provides a copy of the self-assessment instrument you can reproduce and re-use. Job Aid 2.1 is also included in Appendix A.

Another approach is to get others to rate you using the same instrument. This will give you an idea about the degree to which your view of yourself is aligned with how others see you.

If you develop self-assessment as a habit, you will be able over time to see yourself with greater honesty and accuracy.

Self-Reflection

Self-reflection is another method for increasing self-awareness. Self-reflection is the ability to "hit the pause button" and critically assess yourself or a situation.

Importance. Why is self-reflection important to leadership?

- Self-reflection helps you ensure that you are taking actions that are sound and not simply running on "auto pilot," but rather are conscious about doing what is most important in any given situation.

- Self-reflection can help you learn from your experience—to avoid the trap of simply repeating things that aren't working.

- Self-reflection allows you to notice your habitual ways of responding so that you have the option of approaching things differently.

Self-Reflection (Continued)

Methods. There are many ways to reflect, and some methods may work better for you than others. One approach is just to take a short time-out in which you simply stop and think. Other approaches include:

- Journal writing.

- Note taking.

- Talking to others ("thinking out loud").

- Speaking into a tape.

- Meditation.

- Drawing pictures.

Job Aid 2.1 provides guidelines for two of these methods: journal writing and thinking out loud. Give them a try—either now or later, after you have finished this course.

Activity: Self-Reflection

1. Return to the Leadership Behaviors Self-Assessment you completed in Unit 1 (page 1.15).

   The first eight items relate to telescopic behaviors, and the last seven relate to midrange and microscopic behaviors.

   Total your telescopic and midrange/microscopic scores, and enter them below.

	Proficiency	Time Spent	How You Should Apportion Your Time
Telescopic behaviors (Items 1-8)			
Midrange and microscopic behaviors (Items 9-15)			

2. Next, reflect on the following questions:

   - What observations can you make about how your time and abilities differ between the telescopic and midrange/microscopic behaviors?
   - How does this make you think differently about your role as a leader?
   - For your organization or work group to excel, what specific shifts do you need to make in how you spend your time? How will you make these shifts?
   - What skills do you need to strengthen to lead your organization or work group to excellence? How might you go about strengthening those skills?

3. Finally, given your reflections on these questions, reconsider the personal goals you identified at the end of Unit 1. Do you wish to adjust them or add others at this time?

Authentic Feedback

The third technique for increasing self-knowledge is soliciting authentic feedback from others. Leaders who know themselves and let others know them are those who command respect and trust. Soliciting feedback is one of the most effective methods for increasing the open area of the Johari Window, "Known to Self and Others." Feedback is critical to self-knowledge and thus, your ability to lead. It helps you to know if you are leading in ways that are effective for those whom you lead.

Feedback can be informal. We usually think of feedback as a formal process that happens once or twice a year. But you don't have to wait for a formal process to get feedback. In fact, the more informally and frequently you get feedback, the better. It is vital to ask for and receive feedback in a way that encourages others to tell us the truth as they see it.

Feedback requires trust. People may be reluctant to give you honest feedback if they don't trust you. That willingness to be honest is built on trust that develops over time. And to some extent, most of us have a tendency—usually unconscious—to do things that inhibit others from giving us truthful feedback. Down deep, we may not really want the truth.

What can you do to encourage others to give you their honest feedback? On the next page are some tips for encouraging authentic feedback.

<u>Authentic Feedback (Continued)</u>

Tips for Encouraging Authentic Feedback

- Before you ask for feedback, be clear in your own mind why you're asking.

- Ask for feedback only when you are open to hearing it.

- Listen to what they have to say. Take notes.

- Avoid being defensive. Don't try to explain yourself during the feedback process.

- Restate what the speaker has told you, to make sure that you understand what they've said.

- Ask follow-up questions to gain clarity; get specifics. For example:

    - "Can you give me some specifics?"
    - "What impact is that having?"
    - "Can you tell me more about that?"

- Thank them.

- When possible, make changes as a result of the feedback.

- Initially, ask infrequently until others see that you're willing to make changes based on earlier feedback given you. Remember that you need to build trust in the fact that you really *want* to hear what they have to say and that you *will* do something to change.

Remember, those acting out of the Leader paradigm are leaders of change. The best way you can model to others that change is welcome is to grow and change yourself. Soliciting feedback is one of the best ways to show symbolically the people you lead that you are open to input and willing to change. Then, take action on the feedback that you feel is valid.

You are not required to adopt every bit of feedback that people give you. But try thinking about feedback as similar to the gifts you receive for your birthday. To some of them, you'll say, "YES! GREAT!" To others, you'll say, "Thank you," and put them in your closet. Nevertheless, you will benefit more if you stay open to all of the feedback, consider it carefully and with an open mind, and incorporate what seems valid.

Activity: Authentic Feedback

1. Identify at least three people from whom you can solicit authentic feedback about your leadership. They may be subordinates, those with more authority than you, peers, or others. If possible, try to identify people who can offer different perspectives on your leadership.

2. Jot down notes about your feedback strategy—e.g., good situations in which to invite their feedback, timing, lead questions, areas of your leadership you hope to learn more about from this person, and so on.

Feedback Source #1: _____

Strategy:

Feedback Source #2: _____

Strategy:

Feedback Source #3: _____

Strategy:

Understanding How You Think

In the last section, we talked about receiving feedback without explaining or defending yourself. Have you ever noticed what happens when you *really* listen to another person without intending to respond? Perhaps not, because most of us listen only rarely. Usually what we hear is received through many filters, including:

- Assumptions and biases.

- Resistances and barriers stemming from a different set of beliefs.

- Preoccupation with identifying areas of agreement with our own beliefs, and the significance of such agreement.

- Thinking about how we will respond.

Sometimes it's difficult to differentiate between what a person actually says and how we interpret what they said. In other words, our own beliefs affect what and how we hear.

Ladder of Inference

Business theorist Chris Argyris developed a model that explains our thinking process as we interact with the world. This seven-step process, called the Ladder of Inference, is illustrated on the next page. According to this model, as we move up the ladder our beliefs affect what we infer about what we observe and therefore become part of how we experience our interaction with other people.

Ladder of Inference (Continued)

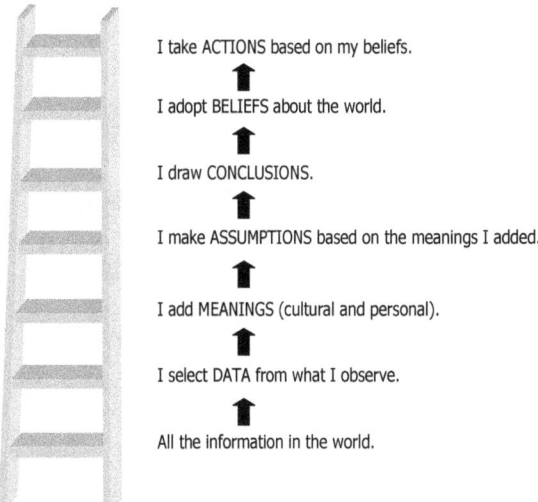

I take ACTIONS based on my beliefs.

⬆

I adopt BELIEFS about the world.

⬆

I draw CONCLUSIONS.

⬆

I make ASSUMPTIONS based on the meanings I added.

⬆

I add MEANINGS (cultural and personal).

⬆

I select DATA from what I observe.

⬆

All the information in the world.

An obvious example of this would be only "hearing" that which supports your own argument. But the process is usually much more subtle. Your background influences the meanings that you ascribe to what you hear, which in turn leads you to make assumptions. In fact, your beliefs affect which data you select in the first place.

If you take the time to "walk" down the Ladder of Inference, you can learn a great deal about how your own beliefs, assumptions, background, culture, and other influences (i.e., your own personal paradigm) affect how you interpret what others say and how you interact with them. It is also a useful tool for reaching a better understanding of those you lead.

Activity: Ladder of Inference

To walk down your Ladder of Inference, try this:

1. Look at the front page of your daily newspaper, and pick a story.

2. Read the story, then answer this question:

   - At lunch, one of your colleagues asks, "So, what do you think about [the topic of the story you selected]?" How would you respond? (At this point, don't overanalyze; just respond.)

3. Next, think about how you arrived at your response. Consider these questions:

   - What made you select that particular story? Did the headline tie in with strong opinions or past experience on your part?
   - What beliefs or opinions did you already hold, related to this topic, before you read the story?
   - What kinds of assumptions did you make as you read the story (For example, if people were quoted, did you believe them? Why or why not?)?
   - How did those assumptions affect the conclusions that you drew about the story?
   - Did your conclusions differ in any way from opinions that you already held?

Creating a Leadership Environment

We talked earlier about one approach that fosters an environment of leadership—soliciting authentic feedback and responding to that feedback with openness to change.

The Ladder of Inference is also a useful tool for creating a leadership environment.

Tips: Using the Ladder of Inference to Create an Environment of Leadership

As you interact with other people, try walking down the ladder to gain a better understanding of how you—and they—think.

- Listen carefully to what people actually say. Try not to interpret at first.

- Listen for conclusions and beliefs—yours and theirs.

  - Do they jump to conclusions?
  - What conclusions are you making as you listen?

- Listen for directly observable data.

  - Can you form a picture in your mind of what they are saying?
  - Ask yourself: What led them to think as they do?

- Suspend your certainties and conclusions.

  - Do they act as if their conclusions are obvious?
  - Do you?
  - Are there other ways of seeing things?

- What must be the Ladder of Inference in their minds?

Inquiry vs. Advocacy

What happens when you sit down with another person or a group of people and discuss something (an issue, a plan, a goal, a problem)? A healthy discussion will include first inquiry, then advocacy.

- **Inquiry.** Inquiry involves talking with other people and *learning* from them. At this stage, you are not judging, arguing, or trying to present your own viewpoint—just learning.

  During this phase you should strive not only to hear the other person's words, but to learn about their mental models to understand where they are coming from and what they are really saying.

  This is also a time for observing your own thoughts, checking out your Ladder of Inference. Inquiry requires that you suspend assumptions. This does not mean laying them aside, but rather bringing them forward and making them explicit so that you and the others can explore their meaning and impact.

- **Advocacy.** A second aspect of communication, after the inquiry stage, is advocacy. Advocacy involves "selling" an idea or position or directing attention to certain facts you think are relevant. This is when you begin to evaluate ideas, narrow the field, and work toward consensus.

In a team context, inquiry and advocacy are sometimes called *dialogue* and *discussion*. During the dialogue phase, everyone should be in an inquiry mode—sharing facts, ideas, and opinions, without evaluating or defending them. By the time you move to the discussion phase, everyone should have a common understanding of all of the facts and viewpoints. Then comes discussion, when you try to determine what you believe in.

The problem in many teams is that they tend to move too quickly to discussion, without adequate inquiry. This has the effect of stifling creative thinking and undermining trust.

Balancing Inquiry and Advocacy

The key—both within yourself and in working with a team—is to balance inquiry and advocacy. You need both.

In your efforts to develop self-knowledge, be aware of your *intentions* behind your inquiry and advocacy, and strive to balance the two. Then, work to enable your group to do the same. Here are some suggestions.

Tips for Balancing Inquiry and Advocacy

- Become aware of the gap between what you intend and what you actually do. (Notice other people's reactions to you: Are they what you expected? Why or why not?) Make an effort to understand and begin to close this gap.

- Let go of the win/lose mindset of controlled discussion. Decide to learn from others.

- Make your thinking visible, and ask others to do the same. State your assumptions, explain your reasoning, and give examples.

- Avoid defensiveness when your ideas are questioned.

- Be aware when you or others are jumping to conclusions.

- Gently walk others down the Ladder of Inference and find out what data they are operating from. Use unaggressive language (e.g., "Can you help me understand your thinking here?").

- Listen without resistance. Hear ideas as if for the first time.

- Respect differences.

- Suspend role and status during dialogue; let leadership become a shared responsibility of the whole group.

- Try to bring forward people who have not spoken, and prompt them to add their views.

- Take risks by participating and being willing to make mistakes. Speak from your own experience.

Balancing Inquiry and Advocacy (Continued)

- When advocating, stay open and encourage others to give different views.

- If you notice that a discussion is lopsided, let the group know what you've observed. Help the group to balance inquiry and advocacy by making your own contributions in a way that creates more balance.

Activity: Your Inner Leader

1. Think about a specific group that you are responsible for leading. In the Johari Window below, fill in the following information:

   a. Open Area: Things about you that are known both to you and to the group.

   b. Hidden Area: Things about you that you know but the group doesn't know.

   Try to list at least five things in each area.

JOHARI WINDOW

	Known to Self	**Unknown to Self**
Known to Others	Open Area	Blind Area
Unknown to Others	Hidden Area	Unknown Area

Activity: Your Inner Leader (Continued)

2. Identify at least one item in your hidden area that, if brought into the open area (i.e., making it known to the group), could improve your effectiveness as a leader.

3. What would be a good way to make this trait known to the group?

4. What are some strategies you can use to learn about what lies in your Blind Area?

5. Review the personal goals that you recorded in the first unit. Add at least one new goal, based on what you have learned in this unit.

Summary and Transition

In this unit, you learned about the importance of self-knowledge as a resource for effective leadership. You learned about paradigms that guide thinking—specifically three leadership paradigms: the Hired Hand, Broker, and Leader paradigms. You also examined the Johari Window as a visual way to think about self-knowledge and explored ways to increase self-knowledge through self-assessment, self-reflection, and soliciting authentic feedback. Finally, you reviewed the concept of the Ladder of Inference and its relationship to inquiry and advocacy and reviewed strategies for balancing inquiry and advocacy.

In Unit 3, you will learn about the leader's role in facilitating change.

For More Information

FEMA EMI Independent Study Course IS-242: *Effective Communication*

Search keywords:
- Leadership in organizations
- Traits of managers and leaders, leadership trends
- Mental models

Knowledge Check

Carefully read each question and all of the possible answers before selecting the most appropriate response for each test item. Circle the letter corresponding to the answer that you have chosen. Complete all of the questions without looking at the course material.

1. Those working out of the Leader paradigm derive credibility and power from:

   a. Reputation for technical proficiency.
   b. Behavioral integrity and core values.
   c. Organizational position and credentials.
   d. Ability to get things done.

2. A likely outcome of increased self-knowledge is:

   a. Vulnerability to self-doubt.
   b. Greater understanding of your intentions by those you lead.
   c. Ability to compensate for your weaknesses.
   d. Greater dependence on external sources of power.

3. If you expand the open area of your Johari Window, you increase:

   a. What others know about you and what you know about yourself.
   b. What is hidden from others about yourself.
   c. What you know about yourself but hide from others.
   d. What you know about everyone else.

4. When soliciting authentic feedback as a means of increasing self-knowledge:

   a. You should set up the feedback session as part of a formal process.
   b. You should carefully explain yourself on each point that is raised.
   c. Every suggested change must be implemented to demonstrate your sincerity.
   d. It is good to restate the feedback and ask follow-up questions.

5. Allowing your beliefs and assumptions to affect how you interpret what someone says is:

   a. An example of the Leader paradigm.
   b. A rare occurrence among those in leadership roles.
   c. An example of the Ladder of Inference.
   d. Not important if you balance inquiry and advocacy.

6. During the inquiry phase of a discussion, you should:

   a. Make your thinking visible and ask others to do the same.
   b. Set discussion ground rules based on role and status.
   c. Adopt a win/lose mindset to better control the discussion.
   d. Challenge others' ideas to generate debate.

Knowledge Check (Continued)

1. b
2. c
3. a
4. d
5. c
6. a

Job Aid 2.1: Self-Reflection Techniques

Journal Writing

Journal writing is one technique for self-reflection. Approached in the right way, it can be a process of *discovery* rather than mere *reporting*. Productive journal writing takes very little time and can be of great benefit. It can be a powerful tool for reflection, self-discovery, problem solving, learning, and integration. Here's how it works:

1. Think about a situation at work with which you are currently struggling or feeling unsettled. (This technique is also good for situations in your personal life.)

2. Write down a set of questions you want to reflect on concerning the situation. Put each question on a separate page, to allow lots of room to write. For starters, try these questions:

   a. What about this situation is uncomfortable or difficult for me?
   b. What did I learn about myself and/or the situation?
   c. What are all of the possible steps I can think of to take, based on what I've just learned?

   As you become familiar with this technique, you can vary the questions to accommodate your own needs for personal growth.

3. Decide on a time limit (for example, 3 minutes per question). If possible, set a timer so you don't have to watch the time.

4. Begin writing. Write about the first question *continuously* for the allotted time. Write whatever comes to your mind. Don't worry about grammar or punctuation. Just *do not stop writing* until the time is up.

5. Respond in the same manner, writing continuously, to each question.

Try this technique every day for a week before you decide whether this approach is a good one for you.

Job Aid 2.1: Self-Reflection Techniques (Continued)

Thinking Out Loud

Thinking out loud is another self-reflection technique. It is quite simple and can be done with a partner or alone, using a tape recorder. These are the ground rules:

1. The partner has only one role: to listen. He or she should not provide suggestions, advice, or insert him- or herself at all in the speaker's process.

2. Select a situation with which you are currently struggling or feeling unsettled, which you will talk about.

3. You may wish to set up a timeframe in advance (e.g., 1 minute to set the context and 4 minutes to speak).

4. Talk.

5. Afterwards, review what you said: Either discuss it with your partner or replay your tape. Many people find that having a "sounding board"—someone to listen without trying to solve their problem—unleashes their creative problem-solving abilities.

Unit 3: Facilitating Change

Introduction

We learned in the previous units that a leader is someone who sets direction and influences people to follow that direction. Someone working out of the Leader paradigm is able to determine a course for change in the future, articulate it as a vision, and stimulate coworkers and self to challenge traditional ways of thinking. The process of becoming a more effective leader often involves personal change—leaving behind some old, comfortable behaviors and considering how to change behaviors that haven't served you well.

In this unit, we will explore the topic of change and how to lead change effectively.

Unit 3 Objectives

After completing this unit, you should be able to:

- Describe key components of the change process.

- Identify methods for effectively communicating about change.

- Identify strategies for facilitating change among employees and other stakeholders.

The Changing Environment

A challenge throughout business, industry, and government today is learning to adapt to the nonstop, rapid changes that are impacting us. In emergency management, change may come in many forms: new policies and procedures, evolving technology and equipment, shifting priorities and issues, increasing community emphasis on mitigation and prevention, new methodologies, and many others. In fact, the whole concept of emergency management implies response to sudden change—often with little warning, but ideally with adequate preparation.

A crucial skill that employees and community members must learn if they are to succeed in today's environment is the ability to respond quickly and effectively to change. An effective leader is able to motivate and inspire others to embrace change.

Four Example Responses to Change

People respond to change in different ways. Take the people in the following story for example:

John, Sarah, David, and Eileen all manage different departments in Springfield County. Budget cuts have just been announced, and the county commissioners want to understand what each of their departments does and have these managers explain why they should continue to receive funding.

Each of these managers' response captures how they feel about change.

- John was angered at yet another round of budget cuts, and instead of providing the requested information, set up a meeting with the county commissioners to argue against them.

- Sarah got to work the moment she received the county commissioners' request, convinced that she would make a convincing case.

- David was initially shocked to hear the news, and spent two days thinking of other possible solutions to the problem before finally settling down and working on the commissioners' request.

- Eileen rationalized that since the county commissioners terms would end within six months, she could stall for time until they, and their request, were hopefully gone.

Self-Reflection Activity: How Have You Responded to Change?

A. Responding to External Change

Think of an instance in which you were faced with a major external change.

1. Can you identify any of the four characters just described in the way that you responded?

2. How did you prepare yourself to make the change?

3. What challenges did you meet along the way?

4. What drove you, or supported you, in making the change?

Self-Reflection Activity: How Have You Responded to Change? (Continued)

B. Responding to Internal Change

What is the most significant *internal* (personal) change that you have ever made?

1. Can you identify any of the four characters in the way that you responded?

2. How did you know that you needed to make the change?

3. How did you prepare yourself to make the change?

4. What challenges did you meet along the way?

5. Who or what drove you, or supported you, in making the change?

What Is at Stake?

Most organizations, whether private or public, have been facing wave after wave of significant change that will only increase in volume, speed, and intensity in the future. With all of the change going on, the cost of failed change has become high for organizations. There is an equally high "human toll" from failed change because the first casualty is loss of trust. Compound that loss with the emergency management goal of protecting life and property in the face of disasters, and the potential loss is great indeed.

Of crucial importance is not **what** change happens, but **how** change happens. In the late 1990s, a study for managing change in the government singled out leadership as the most critical factor in the successful implementation of change. Clearly, organizations that are most successful are those that:

- Have learned how to respond to changes that impact them.

- Have leaders who know how to plan for and implement change well.

- Attend to people's reactions and feelings associated with the change.

Facilitating Change

It is helpful to understand the stages of any change process and what is needed for each to make the process successful.

The stages we will discuss are:

- Defining and Promoting the Change
- Planning and Implementing the Change
- Maintaining the Change
- Engaging People in the Change

These stages are described on the following pages, and it is important to note that this is not a linear process. You will often find yourself working in many stages of the process simultaneously.

Stages of Change

Defining and Promoting the Change

Implementing and managing change is a difficult process. Without a strong, sensible rationale for making the change it will be a struggle to engage staff in the process. People involved need to understand:

- What the change is.
- Why the change is necessary.
- What the change means to them and the organization.
- Why the change needs to happen now.

Defining and promoting the change will help overcome resistance to change and engage people in the process.

The person to successfully lead change needs to have certain characteristics. They need to:

- Be trustworthy, reliable and influential.
- Initiate change but not micromanage or control it.
- Listen to and advocate for both organizational and individual needs.
- Communicate that opportunities are available in the change.
- Maintain public visibility and accessibility during the process.

Stages of Change (Continued)

Planning and Implementing the Change

It is critical to understand the change process, how to effectively manage it, and how to address any problems that could arise.

Planning and implementing the change includes:

- Defining actions and tasks that need to take place to advance the change
- Assigning responsibilities for these actions and tasks
- Creating a time line for the change process
- Dealing with potential problems that may arise along the way, including staff resistance and how to address it
- Defining a means of assessing progress
- Monitoring the impact of the change on staff and the organization
- Developing a feedback loop that can provide information to fine tune the change process as it develops

Critical tools that will be needed for this include:

- Clearly defined policies
- Action and communication plans
- Resources, such as staff training and communications channels

It is vital to include staff with key administrative and organizational authority, as well as those with expertise or technical capacity in these processes to ensure successful adoption by the largest number of staff.

Stages of Change (Continued)

Maintaining Change

It seems odd that change, which is itself an active process, needs to be maintained. However, inertia, resistance, and burnout can all slow, and even stall, the change process.

Maintaining change means:

- Continually engaging those whose support of the process is critical
- Listening to staff concerns and responding to staff needs
- Providing staff what they need, both physical and mental, to support the change

Engaging People in Change

Engaging people in change is largely about maintaining relationships with people during the change process. This includes:

- Asking for feedback during the process
- Accepting a wide range of responses to the change
- Effectively and sincerely responding to the staff feedback and requests

---

Note: Job Aid 3.1 on page 3.16 provides a list of questions that relate to each of the seven components of the process. When applying the process to a change situation that you face, you can use these questions to analyze the situation and develop strategies for effecting change. Job Aid 3.1 is also included in Appendix A.

Activity: Change and the Leadership Paradigms

1. Which of the change process stages just discussed are most associated
   with the Leader paradigm?

2. Which are most associated with the Broker and Hired Hand paradigms?

Activity: Change and the Leadership Paradigms (Continued)

Answers:

1. The following stages relate to the Leader paradigm:

   - Defining and Promoting the Change
   - Maintaining the Change
   - Engaging the People in the Change

2. The following stages relate to the Broker and Hired Hand paradigms:

   - Planning and Implementing the Change
   - Maintaining the Change

Communicating Change

Communication is the common thread that is woven throughout all of the change process components. The ability to communicate effectively about change is a critical aspect of a leader's success at facilitating change.

Many of us have heard of the 5 W's and 1 H of writing a news story (Who, What, When, Where, Why, How). Leaders must effectively communicate the story of change using a reworked version of this. They must explain:

- Why?
- What?
- How?
- Who?

Why?

People need to understand the purpose for the change, and how it relates to the organization's bigger picture.

Key questions might be "What problem are we addressing with this change?" and "What opportunity are we trying to capitalize on?"

What?

A leader must communicate what the future will look like. What will the organization look like? Where will they fit in? The more detailed the information, the better.

How?

Staff must understand what will happen as the plan unfolds. This takes the form of a step-by-step plan of how the change will be carried out, and how and when training and resources to facilitate the change will be distributed.

Who?

Each person involved in the process must understand what their part in the change process will be. How their jobs will change, how they will contribute to the change process, and how they will help define the change process itself.

You may not always have all the information required to communicate the 3 W's and the H. However, it is your responsibility as a leader to get the information needed by those involved in or impacted by change. (Remember, this is the kind of information that enables the "Hems" and "Haws" to move forward.)

Tips for Communicating Change

Here are some additional tips for communicating change.

- **Communicate first through action, then words.**

  In other words, "walk the talk." Your statements, no matter how well crafted, will only deliver a conflicting and ultimately alienating message if your behavior is inconsistent with the underlying values or vision being expressed.

  Behavioral integrity, the hallmark of the Leader paradigm, is of utmost importance when communicating change. As a leader, you are expected to walk the talk and to operate with integrity. If you twist the truth or spin the facts, people will become distrustful and you will lose their respect.

- **Recognize that perceptions will become distorted.**

  During times of change, perceptions become distorted. Employees will read underlying messages into what they see and hear, inferring messages behind actions and statements—even when no message is intended. Keeping people informed and being honest with them go a long way in countering unfounded perceptions.

- **Remember the "rule of six."**

  When people receive new information, they often don't "get it" the first time around, even though we think they should have. That's why it's important to communicate new information related to the change *six times*, in *six different ways*.

- **Anticipate and allow for strong emotions.**

  Allow people to "let off steam." Recognize and communicate that emotions are not only natural, but also a necessary part of the change and transition process. Find productive venues for people to express their anger, frustration, confusion, anxiety, and other emotions.

Summary and Transition

Unit 3 explored the topic of how a leader facilitates change. It described key components of a change process model and identified methods for effectively communicating about change. For change to take place effectively in an organization requires mutual trust between the leader and those who are being encouraged to embrace change. Unit 4 discusses ways to build trust.

Knowledge Check

Carefully read each question and all of the possible answers before selecting the most appropriate response for each test item. Circle the letter corresponding to the answer that you have chosen. Complete all of the questions without looking at the course material.

1. Characteristics of someone to lead change include:

   a. Controlling
   b. Able to initiate change but not micromanage it
   c. Trustworthy, reliable and influential
   d. Both b and c

2. In communicating the purpose of an impending change, it is better to let employees discover the benefits on their own so that they don't build resistance to the change.

   a. True
   b. False

3. Creating an implementation plan, implementing the change, and monitoring the impact of the change are important parts of:

   a. The Jordini Ladder
   b. The change process
   c. Personal response to change
   d. Dealing with disgruntled employees

4. When planning for change, a leader should:

   a. Focus on interim systems because there will be time later to deal with long-term impact.
   b. Consider primarily long-term impacts because the short term will take care of itself.
   c. Include representatives of all key stakeholder groups.
   d. Place the greatest emphasis on how the change will impact the highest levels of management.

5. To sustain energy for change over time, it is important to provide staff with what they need, both physically and mentally, to support the change.

   a. True
   b. False

6. In communicating about change, it is best to discourage the expression of strong emotions among employees to avoid spreading the seeds of doubt.

   a. True
   b. False

Knowledge Check (Continued)

1. d
2. b
3. b
4. c
5. a
6. b

Job Aid 3.1: Change Process Questions

The following questions relate to each of the stages of the change process. When applying the process to a change situation that you face, you can use these questions to analyze the situation and develop strategies for effecting change.

Defining and Promoting the Change

- What must happen for this change to be successful? How should this be communicated to employees or other stakeholders?
- What are the opportunities associated with the change? How can the fear be taken out of the change?
- How can you demonstrate continuous support for, and sponsorship of, this change initiative?
- In what specific ways can you be a catalyst, rather than a controller, of the change?
- What challenges might you encounter in balancing the needs of the organization and those of individuals? How can you manage these challenges?
- How can you "walk the talk" during this change initiative? What pitfalls will you need to avoid?
- What is the rationale for this change? That is, what are we trying to accomplish with the change? How should this be communicated to employees or other stakeholders?
- How can the change initiative be linked to the organization's or the community's strategy, mission, and environment?
- What mechanisms can be used to keep lines of communication with employees and/or stakeholders open and to inform them of progress being made?

Planning and Implementing the Change

- What is the vision for this change—i.e., what would you like to see happen as a result of this change? What do you see as the benefits of the change?
- What are the major components of a plan for this change?
- How can you keep employees and/or stakeholders involved in the process?
- What potential problems and opportunities are associated with this change?
- What existing systems might need to be modified to reinforce needed changes?
- What mechanisms should be put in place for monitoring and evaluating the implementation of the change?
- What potential resistance points might you encounter? How can you manage this resistance?
- How might production be impacted and how can you manage this?
- What resources will be needed to implement this change successfully? How can you secure these resources?
- What interim systems might you need to implement? How should they be implemented?

Job Aid 3.1: Change Process Questions (Continued)

Maintaining the Change

- What formal and informal mechanisms can you use to communicate the change?
- How can you sustain energy and commitment to this change over time?
- Whose support will be critical to the successful implementation of this change? How will you gain their support?
- What might employees and/or stakeholders need to accept and support this change?
- What small successes can you celebrate? How?

Engaging the People in the Change

- What reactions to this change initiative do you anticipate from employees and/or stakeholders?
- What pitfalls should you avoid when responding to these reactions?
- What mechanisms can you use to solicit employee and/or stakeholder concerns? How can you demonstrate that you are listening to their concerns about the change?
- In what ways can you monitor their comments and feedback?

Unit 4: Building and Rebuilding Trust

Introduction

In the last unit, we examined the phenomenon of change, and how an effective leader facilitates change. One of the most striking casualties of change is trust. The speed and frequency of change, and its often unintended consequences, often result in erosion of loyalty and trust that can continue to undermine an organization for years.

The relationship between change and trust is full of irony. You can't effectively facilitate change without mutual trust. But one of the hardest things to do in a changing organization is to build trust. Even more difficult is to rebuild it after it is lost.

In this unit, we will examine the issue of trust and explore ways in which an effective leader can build or rebuild trust among employees and other emergency management stakeholders.

Unit 4 Objectives

After completing this unit, you should be able to:

- Describe the role of trust as it relates to emergency management.

- Examine your personal capacity to trust and to generate trust.

- Identify behaviors that build trust or mistrust.

- Develop strategies for building or rebuilding trust in your own leadership situation.

What Is Trust?

Trust is a relationship based on mutual confidence that we will both:

- Do what we say.

- Communicate honestly.

- Respect one another's knowledge, skills, and abilities.

- Maintain confidentiality.

- Keep our interactions unguarded.

Trust is a state of mind. Notice that all of these things are actions. It's not our words that generate trust, but what we do. The real message is in our actions. Trust is a combination of **trusting others** and **being trustworthy**.

What's So Important About Trust?

Trust is a fundamental building block of human relationships. In simple terms, it's just how people treat each other.

Trust is also the very core of leadership. Willing followers must trust their leaders. (Without trust, no one will follow.) But trust cannot be mandated; it must be earned.

Earlier, we said that people working out of the Leader paradigm get their credibility and power "from behavioral integrity—'walking the talk and talking the walk.' Leaders' power comes from their consistent, principle-centered behavior and actions that demonstrate honesty, integrity, trust, dignity, and respect for all people." This is why people choose to follow them.

Benefits of a High-Trust Environment

A high-trust environment creates commitment and loyalty to the organization. When people get the idea, "We're all in this boat together," the organization is invariably better for it.

In a high-trust environment, leadership tells the truth, and people are enlightened about the organization's position and what actions they need to take to help achieve its goals.

In a high-trust environment, people are more willing to accept change and to work toward successfully integrating the effects of change.

Trust in Emergency Management

Every manager in business, industry, and government has an important leadership role in building a high-trust environment with his or her employees.

As a leader within emergency management, you have a more complex role of building trust at multiple levels. Trust is a necessary element of:

- Leading your subordinates to work energetically toward meeting the organization's goals.

- Developing trusting relationships with other levels of the government hierarchy to ensure a coordinated response to the needs of the community in times of crisis.

- Working with other agencies in joint prevention, preparedness, response, recovery, and mitigation efforts, including evaluation of hazards, planning, inter-agency exercises, and voluntary agreements.

- Teaming with other agencies in disaster response and recovery efforts.

- Developing constructive relationships with the media to ensure effective cooperation in public education, warning, and response communications.

- Building positive relationships with the public that will foster willing response and cooperation during times of emergency.

The effective response to the first World Trade Center bombing was attributed to the years of interagency cooperation, careful evaluation of hazards and planning, and meaningful interagency exercises. This same foundation of trust undoubtedly played an equally important part in the cooperative response efforts that followed the 2001 attack that destroyed the World Trade Center.

In short:

Your relationships with local, State, and Federal officials, with other organizations, with the media, and with the public will affect your ability to manage a disaster successfully. Those relationships are built on a foundation of trust.

Building Trust

When things are continually changing, it can become difficult to build a case for trust. It's almost as if you were saying "Trust me … I've never done this either!"

In these times of rapid change, more than ever before, your challenge as a leader is to build trust where it has never been and to rebuild trust where it has been lost.

Many of the strategies discussed in Unit 3 will help you to minimize the erosion of trust. How else can you, as a leader, build trust among your constituents—whether they are employees, those above you in rank, your peers in other organizations, the media, or the public?

Activity: Trust Behaviors

1. What are some of the specific ways that you demonstrate that you "do what you say"?

2. What are some of the ways you can show respect for the knowledge, skills, and abilities of your employees or other stakeholders?

3. What actions can you take to ensure that your interactions with employees and/or stakeholders are and will remain unguarded?

Activity: Trust Behaviors (Continued)

Learning Points:

1. Doing what you say may be evidenced by such behaviors as:

   - Managing expectations
   - Establishing boundaries
   - Delegating appropriately
   - Encouraging mutually serving intentions
   - Honoring agreements
   - Being consistent
   - Meeting expectations

2. You can demonstrate respect for other people's knowledge, skills, and abilities by such actions as:

   - Acknowledging their abilities to do their jobs.
   - Allowing them to use their talents to accomplish goals.
   - Being aware of your control needs and their impact on others.
   - Reducing controls; not micromanaging.
   - Involving others and seeking their input.
   - Helping people learn skills.
   - Giving them the resources, authority, and responsibility needed to get their work done right.
   - Trusting your own competence to assess each situation with open eyes and determine whom you can trust with what.

3. You can demonstrate unguarded interactions by such behaviors as:

   - Sharing information.
   - Telling the truth.
   - Admitting mistakes.
   - Giving and receiving constructive feedback.
   - Allowing for mutual influence; clarifying mutual expectations.
   - Maintaining confidentiality.
   - Speaking with good purpose.

Building and Nurturing Trust

Building and nurturing trust in the workplace requires leaders who:

- Honestly describe any situation they are in, including discussing any loss of trust that has occurred.
- Respect others and relationships with them during tough times as well as when things are smooth sailing.
- Nurture understanding and empathy with themselves and with others.
- Desire to build and maintain a cooperative organizational culture.

Are You Trustworthy?

Demonstrating trustworthiness is critical if you want to successfully manage change, and you should periodically gauge how worthy of trust your own behavior is. You can use the following questions as a starting point.

Are You Trustworthy?

- **Is my behavior predictable or erratic?**

  Do people know what to expect from me? Do my actions match the values I espouse? Your actions should follow your words and should stay constant regardless of the times or people you are working with.

- **Do I communicate clearly or carelessly?**

  Some people speak without thinking of the impression their words leave behind and how they impact people's lives. When you speak without considering this, people begin to think you are flippant and not worthy of trust.

- **Do I keep my promises?**

  If you don't keep your promises, then neither will those you work with. If people cannot tell what you value and will follow through on, confusion and mistrust will result.

- **Am I forthright or dishonest?**

  No one trusts someone who lies. Honesty doesn't mean that you disclose everything when it isn't appropriate, but you need to be honest about what you can and cannot discuss.

What Is Your Capacity for Trust?

Your ability to trust others reflects to some extent your ability to trust yourself.

The following questions will help you begin to think about your capacity for trusting others.

Questions about Your Capacity for Trust

- **Do you trust yourself?**

    - In what types of situations can you answer "yes" and in which is the answer "no"?
    - In what ways do you consider yourself reliable?
    - In what ways do you consider yourself unreliable?

- **Do you trust others?**

    - When can you say "yes" to this? When do you say "no"?
    - What do you look for when considering whether another person is trustworthy?

- **Do you trust people as a habit, or do you wait for them to prove themselves?**

    - How does this affect how you work with others?

Deciding to Trust

Your capacity for building trusting relationships, in general, is a function of your propensity to use trust-enhancing behaviors and the degree to which you expect others to use them.

But what about specific relationships? Your decision to trust a specific person, and the degree of trust that you place in that person, are influenced by many factors, including:

- History and experience with that individual.

- The person's level of competence and ability.

- How much risk is involved, or the potential for negative consequences.

- The person's relative power and authority.

- The organizational environment.

So, you can work diligently on your general propensity to trust, but some people will still let you down. Does that mean that you shouldn't trust?

No, because although trust can be person-specific and situation-specific, you still have a general propensity to (or not to) trust. And that propensity will in turn influence the decisions that you make. Most people can stand to expand their capacity for trust.

Expanding Your Capacity for Trust

First, you can simply **be aware** of the kinds of behaviors that help to build and maintain interpersonal trust, including those that you personally tend to (or not to) demonstrate.

Then, you can **identify instances, examples, and situations** where you can try to use those trusting behaviors (that you might not use enough) more frequently.

Activity: Reflecting on Your Trust Behaviors

1. Reflect on the "Are You Trustworthy?" exercise (page 4.8). Then, list at least one action that you can take to improve in each of the following areas:

   a. To improve the predictability of my behavior, I can:

   b. To improve the clarity of my communication, I can:

   c. To improve the seriousness with which I treat my promises, I can:

   d. To improve my forthrightness, I can:

2. Reflect on the Questions about Your Capacity for Trust (page 4.9). In what ways or in what situations do you have the **least** capacity for trust?

Trust-Reducing Behaviors

We have discussed a number of ways to build trust and fulfill the expectations of a trusting relationship: doing what we say; communicating honestly; respecting one another's knowledge, skills, and abilities; maintaining confidentiality; and keeping our interactions unguarded.

Just as consistently fulfilling expectations strengthens trust, failure to act in these ways invariably undermines and erodes trust. For example, the following types of behavior will invariably reduce trust:

- Distorting, withholding, or concealing real motives.

- Falsifying relevant information.

- Attempting to control or dominate.

- Not discussing or meeting others' expectations of performance or behavior.

- Attempting to evade responsibility for behavior.

- Accepting credit for other people's work.

- Not honoring commitments.

- Gossiping.

Any of these behaviors can be intentional or unintentional.

Remember, building trust is a slow process, and trust can be destroyed by a single event. Trust is destroyed by a win/lose mentality, and trust is strengthened by a win/win mentality.

Activity: Trust vs. Mistrust

Instructions: Review each of the following behaviors. Decide if it would be likely to build trust or to build mistrust. Then, check the appropriate box.

Behavior	Builds Trust	Builds Mistrust
1. When in doubt about taking on a commitment, air your concerns with the relevant parties.	☐	☐
2. Be unclear or not exactly explicit about what you need or expect. Assume that anyone would know to do or not do that.	☐	☐
3. Solve problems through direct communication at the lowest equivalent levels: yourself and peers; yourself and your direct manager; yourself, your manager, and his/her manager.	☐	☐
4. When engaged in an ongoing commitment, communicate anticipated slippage as soon as you suspect it.	☐	☐
5. Make a pretended or "soft" commitment (e.g., "I'll respond later.").	☐	☐
6. Schedule regular meetings for input and feedback for those reporting to you.	☐	☐
7. Acknowledge the intent and risk of innovation first, then address the issue with your honest opinion.	☐	☐
8. Talk with others about problems you are having with a peer, without doing everything reasonably possible to solve the problem through direct communication with that peer.	☐	☐
9. Spend "informal" time mingling, asking nonassumptive questions, making only promises you can keep, and working back through existing lines of authority.	☐	☐
10. Take credit for yourself, or allow others to give you credit for an accomplishment that was not all yours.	☐	☐
11. Communicate abruptly when others venture new opinions or efforts.	☐	☐
12. Have performance evaluation time be the only, or primary, time for coaching input.	☐	☐
13. Engage in tactful, direct communication, airing your problem and seeking win-win resolution.	☐	☐
14. Withhold deserved recognition at times when you, yourself, are feeling underrecognized.	☐	☐

Activity: Trust vs. Mistrust (Continued)

Behavior	Builds Trust	Builds Mistrust
15. Manage or supervise from behind your desk only.	☐	☐
16. Share credit generously. When in doubt, share.	☐	☐
17. Be explicit and direct. If compromise is productive, do it in communication, not in your mind alone.	☐	☐
18. Be timely.	☐	☐
19. Be willing to be wrong.	☐	☐
20. Withhold potentially useful information, opinions, or action until the drama heightens, thus minimizing your risk of being wrong and maximizing credit to you if you're right.	☐	☐
21. Hold in your mind another department's productivity or behavior as a reason for less cooperation.	☐	☐
22. Extend yourself beyond your own short-term feeling and validate success or new effort.	☐	☐
23. Develop systems for staff to evaluate supervisors and managers.	☐	☐

Activity: Trust vs. Mistrust (Continued)

Answers:

	Builds Trust	Builds Mistrust
1.	✓	
2.		✓
3.	✓	
4.	✓	
5.		✓
6.	✓	
7.	✓	
8.		✓
9.	✓	
10.		✓
11.		✓
12.		✓
13.	✓	
14.		✓
15.		✓
16.	✓	
17.	✓	
18.	✓	
19.	✓	
20.		✓
21.		✓
22.	✓	
23.	✓	

When Trust Breaks Down

You'll probably survive one unintentional breach of trust, especially if you take action to address the situation. But as unintentional breaches accumulate, other people will eventually begin to distrust you. With their distrust will come the belief that your intentions are not sincere and that you have ulterior motives.

Restoring Breached Trust

After you've breached trust, it is important to consider how to restore it. Here are six steps that you can take to recover from a mistake that may have unintentionally damaged trust.

- **Accept:** Accept personal responsibility for your actions and those of your organization.

- **Admit:** Publicly acknowledge that you have made a mistake. Many times, leaders either deny or attempt to cover up any wrongdoing for fear that admitting a mistake might damage their credibility. Evidence shows that attempting to hide mistakes will be much more damaging and will actually erode trust.

- **Apologize:** Offer an apology. This lets others know that you are concerned about the impact or problem that your actions may have created.

- **Act:** Take action to deal with the immediate consequences of a mistake. This lets employees know that you are willing to do something. This is a good time to get others involved by asking for suggestions and trusting their judgment.

- **Amend:** Make amends. A leader's error can cause undue hardship to others. The amends should fit the problem.

- **Attend:** Leaders need to make sure that they are attuned to the influence their actions are having on rebuilding lost trust. Pay close attention to the reactions of those who are affected, ask for feedback, and be nondefensive in listening to constructive criticism. This should also help you avoid unintentional breaches of trust in the future.

Case Study 4.1: The Grapevine

Read the following case study about a breakdown in trust. Then, answer the questions that follow.

Jonas Wale heads up the Logistics department at an emergency response organization. When he assumed the position a year ago, he encountered numerous personnel problems that distracted employees' energies from the agency's mission. Since then, he has worked to change the culture and has had some success in redirecting the efforts of the department. He established clear expectations and timelines, and he has given people clear and ongoing feedback on their performance. He also instituted regular staff meetings in which there is an open exchange of ideas, and he has implemented a number of the employees' ideas. Jonas prides himself on being open, honest, and fair with those in his department and has been forthright with his own supervisor, Gepetta Klinger, division director for Operations.

Two employees, Syd and Ima, stop by and tell Jonas what they heard at lunch. A couple of team leaders from the other department in their division said they had heard that senior management had decided to go with a new software package that Logistics had been testing. The package will be used in deployment and tracking of emergency resources (including personnel, equipment, supplies, volunteers, shelter space, and donations) as well as purchasing and replacement. The decision was made despite the department's recommendation to the contrary because of bugs in the program. They also heard that there would be staffing cuts throughout the division to pay for the software and take advantage of the efficiencies it's supposed to create.

Jonas had heard several months ago that the package would undergo further testing, and he hadn't heard much about it since. So he tells Syd and Ima that it's probably all speculation and that there's no truth to the rumors. When they continue to question his thinking, he forcefully argues that, if it were true, he would have heard about it long before they did because of how well connected he is with the division's decisionmakers. Syd and Ima are still skeptical, but they accept his perspective and go back to their tasks.

The next day, the software implementation and its impact on division personnel comes up in a staff meeting, and Jonas again disputes the "rumors," wondering aloud why it has caused such a stir now. He calms the group by agreeing to check it out with his supervisor. When he tries to do so, he finds that she is out the rest of the week. So, he tells the staff that he'll let them know when he finds out more.

Gepetta, Jonas's supervisor, calls during the weekend and tells him that early last week the Executive Committee decided that they needed to go with the new package because the "price was too good to be true." The vendor offered a huge discount in exchange for a quick decision. When the organization hesitated during negotiations, the vendor offered to upgrade the software as needed over the next 5 years.

Gepetta asks Jonas to "keep a lid" on the announcement until senior management can put together an organization-wide announcement—hopefully, by Wednesday. Part of the announcement will be a 15 percent reduction in division staffing over the next year. Jonas explains that word is out already, that he's been hearing about it through the grapevine. Gepetta apologizes for not letting him know earlier, and expresses dismay with the organization's inability to "manage" these communications, and relief that no one in her division caused it.

Continued . . .

Case Study 4.1: The Grapevine (Continued)

On Monday, Jonas and Gepetta talk further. She says that, while the new package has some problems, the vendor is strong and very committed to working them out. She sees the change as an opportunity to:

- Improve public safety through quicker deployment of needed resources.
- Save money by reducing the number of staff required to run and support the program.
- Upgrade the expertise of the employees as they learn and train others on the new software.
- Improve overall efficiency and communications among the various departments.
- Lighten the workload of division employees who previously have had to do a lot of manual tracking and recording.

She sees a "natural fit" for Jonas's department to "join hands" with the other department. While this makes sense on paper, historically there has been little cooperation between the two departments, mainly because the other department has a reputation for poor service and low morale.

On Tuesday, Syd drops by and asks Jonas if he has any answers yet. Jonas tells him what he knows (i.e., he spills the beans). Through the rest of the day, he visits with the staff and passes on, in general terms, the same information.

Questions:

1. What instances of trust building do you see in this situation?

2. Where are the breakdowns in trust in this situation? What behaviors contributed to mistrust?

Case Study 4.1: The Grapevine (Continued)

3. How could the situation have been handled differently to preserve or build trust?

Case Study 4.1: The Grapevine (Continued)

Key Learning Points:

1. Trust-building behaviors included:

   - Jonas's establishing clear expectations and timelines, providing clear and ongoing feedback, running open staff meetings, and implementing suggested changes.
   - Syd's and Ima's sharing what they heard with Jonas.
   - Jonas's honesty in sharing with his employees information that will affect them professionally.

2. The most obvious breach of trust is Jonas's breaking of Gepetta's confidence. The real betrayal occurs, however, when decisions that affect people's lives are carried out without awareness of, and sensitivity to, their impact. In choosing not to have an open exchange of information within the organization, senior management undermines trust. Gepetta's failure to inform Jonas in a timely manner, then creating for him a moral dilemma by asking him to "keep the lid on," forces him to lose trust one way or another—either betray her confidence or betray his employees. Beyond the internal issues of the organization, the public's trust has been betrayed if management has let itself be pressured into a compromise with "poor performance" to get a good price. Other trust-eroding behaviors included:

   - Jonas's preoccupation with his own "connectedness" that leads him to discount Syd's and Ima's input and be defensive when they disagree.
   - Gepetta's interest in "managing" communications rather than dealing honestly with employees.
   - Gepetta's putting forth the need for damage-control measures as interdepartmental cooperation.
   - Jonas's using the other department's problems as an excuse for less cooperation.

3. Although there are various ways in which each of the actors could improve the climate of trust through their behavior, the foundation of mistrust in the organization limits the range of trust-building alternatives for all concerned. Within his own unit, Jonas can work toward rebuilding trust by:

   - Accepting responsibility for his actions and those of the organization.
   - Admitting that his own self-view let him be taken by surprise in this situation, and apologize.
   - Take action to deal with the consequences with his department.
   - Communicate openly with employees about the situation and its impact (both on employees and on the climate of trust), and attend to their concerns.

Activity: Building Trust in Your Situation

Think of a recent situation in your work in which trust was a factor (e.g., a change initiative within your organization, dealings with the media, response—or lack of response—by the public in an emergency, or a team effort with other agencies). With this situation in mind, answer the following questions.

1. What actions were taken (or could be taken) to strengthen trust (or at least not compromise it)?

2. In what ways and under what circumstances (either intentional or unintentional) might you have caused or reinforced mistrust during this situation?

Activity: Building Trust in Your Situation (Continued)

3. Based on this analysis, what actions can you take to build and rebuild trust in the future?

4. Based on this analysis, what actions can others (i.e., coworkers, team members, and/or senior management) take to build and rebuild trust in the future?

Summary and Transition

Unit 4 examined the issue of trust, and explored ways in which an effective leader can build or rebuild trust among employees and other emergency management stakeholders. Unit 5 discusses how personal influence and political savvy enter into a leader's effectiveness.

For More Information

Books:

- *Building Trust at the Speed of Change.* Marshall, Edward M. 1999.

- *Trust and Betrayal in the Workplace.* Reina, Dennis, and Reina, MIchelle. Berrett-Koehler Pub., 1999.

- *Building Trust: A Manager's Guide for Business Success.* Shurtleff, Mary. Crisp Publications, 1998.

- *Driving Fear out of the Workplace: Creating the High-Trust, High-Performance Organization.* Ryan, Kathleen, and Oestreich, Daniel K. Jossey-Bass, 1998.

Knowledge Check

Carefully read each question and all of the possible answers before selecting the most appropriate response for each test item. Circle the letter corresponding to the answer that you have chosen. Complete all of the questions without looking at the course material.

1. Which of the following is a good way to demonstrate respect for other people's skills:

   a. Micromanaging
   b. Making excuses for their inability to meet deadlines
   c. Seeking their input
   d. Giving them responsibility without authority

2. Demonstrating conviction, courage, compassion, and community can:

   a. Undermine or erode trust.
   b. Make you vulnerable to your adversaries.
   c. Be used to build trust.
   d. Diminish your capacity for trust.

3. The capacity for trusting others is inborn and cannot be changed.

   a. True
   b. False

4. The degree to which you trust yourself can affect your capacity to trust others.

   a. True
   b. False

5. Withholding your real motives is an example of:

   a. Trust-reducing behavior
   b. Shrewd management technique
   c. Trust-building behavior
   d. Keeping things under wraps

6. Airing your concerns about taking on a commitment is likely to:

   a. Reduce your responsibility but enhance your authority.
   b. Erode trust.
   c. Expand your capacity to trust.
   d. Build trust.

7. In a high-trust environment, people are more willing to accept change.

   a. True
   b. False

Knowledge Check (Continued)

1. c
2. c
3. b
4. a
5. a
6. d
7. a

Unit 5: Personal Influence and
Political Savvy

Introduction

In addition to building trust and facilitating change, an effective leader must be able to exert personal influence to achieve emergency management goals. In this unit, we will focus on the important role of leader as influencer and the skills for effectively influencing others. We will also explore what is involved in being a politically savvy leader.

Unit 5 Objectives

After completing this unit, you should be able to:

- Recognize the need for and importance of using personal influence.

- Identify the key aspects of political savvy.

- Develop strategies for influencing individuals, groups, and the organization to a specific course of action.

Personal Influence and Emergency Management

What does personal influence have to do with emergency management? To illustrate, let's begin with a case study.

Read and analyze the following case study: where do you think personal influence plays a part in the emergency manager's job?

Case Study 5.1: Findlay City Fiasco

Jane Canfield is the emergency manager in Findlay City. Last month, the city experienced a disaster. A flash flood inundated the city with water that threatened to overtake the entire downtown area. Because of the massive force of the flood waters, a levee burst on the outskirts of the city. To compound matters, a hazardous chemical spill closed a major thoroughfare into the city. The spill was releasing toxic fumes into the area and HazMat experts determined that the 100 homes immediately surrounding the accident should be evacuated.

At the time of the disaster, the city had a new mayor who did not yet understand his role in emergency management, so he failed to act quickly to issue an evacuation order. When the delayed evacuation order was issued, the media broadcast it on all TV stations but did not continue the broadcast on the Spanish language station that most Hispanics rely on for their evening news. The outdoor warning system failed in several areas, but people heard the police cars' sirens and figured that something was wrong. Five people died of respiratory failure as a result of the delay and confusion.

Massive convergence of spectators downtown caused traffic tie-ups that delayed rescue personnel trying to reach people stranded by the flood waters. The flood caused 14 deaths, 12 of them in a mobile home park. The city council had voted down enforcing the building codes that would have required more reinforcement for mobile homes to protect them against damage.

The emergency manager handled the resource requirements with the assistance of the neighboring jurisdictions, which provided additional fire and rescue support. There was confusion in some agencies about interagency policy and protocol, however, which caused some delays and created an impression of disorganization and lack of cooperation.

Meanwhile, the media sensationalized the story, reported that the city was overwhelmed by the impact, and did nothing to reassure the public.

Continued . . .

Case Study 5.1: Findlay City Fiasco (Continued)

Looking back on the incident, Canfield realizes there are many ways in which the city can improve its ability to deal with another disaster. She is drafting an action plan that, so far, includes the following items:

- Meet with the mayor to brief him on hazard analysis, the emergency operations plan, authorities and responsibilities, and emergency management statutes and develop a closer working relationship.

- Work with city council, the zoning board, and other appropriate agencies to review existing building code standards and regulations regarding development in hazardous areas.

- Meet with local businesses and trade associations to discuss recovery issues and develop interest in hazard mitigation programs.

- Cultivate local government and community commitment to emergency management.

- Identify organizations and individuals to contact on a regular basis to establish or maintain informal working relationships.

- Identify ways to meet the needs of special populations in the event of a disaster.

- Identify ways to rebuild public trust in Findlay City's emergency management program.

- Implement public education and awareness campaigns about the hazards that exist in the community and ways to prepare for them.

- Cultivate a positive working relationship with the media to ensure effective early warning systems and unbiased reporting of emergency events.

- Work with those responsible for the outdoor warning system to ensure effective performance in the future.

- Initiate a review of policies and procedures with response groups to ensure future coordination and cooperation.

Case Study 5.1: Findlay City Fiasco (Continued)

Question: What opportunities do you see for the emergency manager to use personal influence in improving the city's approach to emergency management?

Personal Influence and Emergency Management (Continued)

The ability to influence others is a key leadership competency. At a minimum, we use our influencing skills to get needed resources and set people on a particular course of direction.

As you probably noticed in the case study, personal influence is absolutely critical in emergency management. Every one of the tasks that the emergency manager outlined in her action plan will require some measure of personal influence, and those tasks cover the entire emergency management spectrum: prevention, preparedness, response, recovery, and mitigation.

The emergency manager will need to exercise her influence in many directions:

- Upward (with the mayor).

- Laterally (with other emergency managers in neighboring jurisdictions, city council, the zoning board, and other agencies).

- Downward (with those responsible for various facets of the emergency management program).

- Outward (with the media, the public, businesses, trade organizations, and specific groups such as the Hispanic community).

Personal Influence

When we talk about influencing other people, we generally mean getting them to do something or to think or behave in a certain way.

Three Types of Influence

In the workplace, you have three kinds of influence available to you: position influence, domineering influence, and interpersonal influence.

- **Position influence**

  Position influence is derived from your job position or title. You use your authority to meet your objective. This kind of influence usually results in compliance: employees do what you want because you're their boss. Position influence can be temporary if you are a project head or in charge of a particular assignment.

  The best uses of position influence are when there are strict rules and established procedures, when automatic compliance is required, to recognize and strengthen good performance, and to deal with performance or conduct issues.

- **Domineering influence**

  Domineering influence is usually based on frustration and involves harsh behavior, threats, and elevated tones. The result is often hostility and passive-aggressive behavior. It can destroy working relationships and therefore should only be used when all else fails.

Three Types of Influence (Continued)

- **Interpersonal influence**

  Unlike position or domineering influence, interpersonal influence has to be developed or earned. It does not come with a job title or emotion. You build interpersonal influence as you demonstrate your own qualities and skills, such as good listening and reacting skills, a sense of humor, and reliability. Interpersonal influence is based on trust, support, and collaboration. It results in commitment to the task or purpose: people decide that they want to work with you to get the job done.

  Interpersonal influence is best used:

  - When you have no direct authority over others.
  - When "buy-in" is required.
  - When creativity and two-way information sharing is required.
  - With professionals who expect to be treated with respect and to work collaboratively.
  - For teambuilding.
  - For responding to change.

  Even if you predominantly use one type of influence, you may use all three types with some individuals and groups or in some situations where it is appropriate.

Effective Interpersonal Influence

Interpersonal influence is something you develop over time, as you build relationships. It is also something that you develop as you gain knowledge and experience in your job. The more you know about your organization, the better equipped you are to influence positively those you need to.

Effective interpersonal influence involves three core elements: "I," "You," and "We." Each element reflects an attitude. When you adopt this attitude, you tend to act in a way that contributes to effective interpersonal influence.

- **The "I" element.** This element reflects the attitude, "I am a trustworthy ally." It involves taking actions that demonstrate your personal reliability, competence, and commitment. People learn about you from what you *say* and how you *act*. They will determine whether you are trustworthy based on your actions, and they will notice quickly if your actions do not correspond with your words.

  Examples of actions that can destroy your credibility include:

  - Criticizing people behind their backs.
  - "Passing the buck."
  - Repeating confidential information to others.

  If people decide that you are not trustworthy, a strong barrier will be created to building an influence relationship.

- **The "You" element.** This element reflects the attitude, "You are a valuable resource." Actions that demonstrate this attitude show the other person that you value a working relationship with him or her. Examples include asking for their opinions and ideas and showing appreciation for their contributions.

- **The "We" element.** This element reflects the attitude, "We can accomplish this together." The "I" and "We" elements together enable you to build an influence relationship. After you've done that, you can use the relationship to work together to solve problems and accomplish your goals (the "We" element).

Personal Influence Skills

You have learned about many personal influence skills in previous units. We influence others through our leadership skills, through effective balancing of inquiry and advocacy, through trust-building behaviors, and by being able to communicate change effectively.

Your ability to influence others is also enhanced by effective communication skills, including:

- Effective public speaking and interviewing skills.

- Active listening.

- Attending and encouraging.

- Paraphrasing.

- Reflecting feelings.

- Distinguishing between emotion and content.

To maximize these skills, you may wish to complete the FEMA Independent Study course, *Effective Communication* (course number IS-242).

Negotiating Agreement

Another important skill area in building influence relationships is reacting skills: the ability to react appropriately to another person's point of view after you understand it. The ability to react effectively is important because influence relationships develop when both parties feel that their ideas are important to the other. Reacting effectively encourages open communication and trust.

Typically, there are three gut reactions you may have to someone's idea or suggestion:

- Agree
- Disagree
- Think of ways to enhance the idea

No matter what your gut reaction, the important thing is to react to it in a way that is both honest and maintains a positive climate for future communication. There are three skills that will allow you to do this:

- **Agreeing**

  If you like the person's idea, say so. But make sure you state both *what* you like and *why* you like it. For example, you might say, "I like your idea of . . . because . . . ." By communicating the value that the idea has for you (i.e., why you like it), you give the person additional reinforcement for offering the idea.

- **Constructive Disagreement**

  When people suggest ideas, they hope that their ideas will be liked. But that isn't always the case. Sometimes the response is disagreement. People often find it difficult to state their disagreement, however. Either they don't want to hurt the person's feelings, or they don't like to say "no," or they don't know how to say "no" diplomatically.

  The result is that they sometimes take inappropriate actions, such as postponing giving an answer, going along with an unacceptable idea, or implying that the disagreement stems from someone else (e.g., "I don't think *they* will let us do that").

  If disagreement is not handled correctly, the person can become defensive or the possibility of future discussions may be dampened. The self-esteem of the person should be a major concern.

Negotiating Agreement (Continued)

If your reaction is that you see value in the idea but have some reservations (agree with parts and disagree with others), use constructive disagreement. Here's how:

1. **Identify the value.** For example, you might say, "What I like about your idea is . . . ." If you listened carefully, you'll understand both the idea and why the person thinks that it's a good one. Identifying the value in the idea lets the person know that you are listening, which will help the person hear your concerns.

2. **Explain your reservations.** For example, you might say, "What concerns me is . . . ," or "These are the things that would need to be overcome." Make sure you're specific and clear. And avoid the tendency to jump prematurely to your reservations. Express the value first!

3. **Discuss alternatives.** Talk about ways to retain the value while eliminating reservations. The goal is to modify the original idea so that it is acceptable to both of you. The modifications can come from you or from the other person (i.e., either ask for or offer suggestions). If you offer a suggestion, ask the other person for his or her reaction to it. This keeps the conversation as a two-way dialogue.

- **Building on Ideas**

When your reaction to someone's suggestion is that it stimulates your thinking about the idea and ways to enhance it, you have an opportunity to build on ideas—to add value to the original idea. This does not mean just offering a new idea of your own. There are two steps in this process.

1. **Acknowledge the connection.** First, acknowledge the connection between the person's idea and what you are about to say. For example, you might begin, "What you said about . . . ." This lets the person know that you were listening and gives them credit for the initial idea in the building process.

2. **Add value.** Modify the original idea to add value to it (e.g., suggest additional reasons why the idea is a good one or ways to make the idea even better).

Activity: Negotiating Agreement

In the case study, "The Grapevine," in Unit 4, Syd and Ima reported a conversation to Jonas, and he disagreed with their conclusions about its significance:

> So he tells Syd and Ima that it's probably all speculation and that there's no truth to the rumors. When they continue to question his thinking, he forcefully argues that, if it were true, he would have heard about it long before they did because of how well connected he is with the division's decision makers. Syd and Ima are still skeptical, but they accept his perspective and go back to their tasks.

Using the principles of negotiated agreement, how could Jonas have responded in a more constructive manner?

Activity: Negotiating Agreement (Continued)

Suggested answer:

Jonas's response would have been better if he had:

- Identified the value in their message (appreciation for their sharing the information, acknowledgment of the significance if the message is accurate).

- Expressed his reservations about the reliability of the information.

- Suggested alternatives (people he could talk to, steps he could take).

- Asked for their reactions or suggestions.

While Jonas did some of these things, his response was cut short by his defensiveness, so he did not develop a true two-way dialogue. Rather, he fell back on his position influence instead of using the opportunity to strengthen an influence relationship.

Political Savvy

There are times when the ability to influence others is not enough, and a good rationale may not be sufficient to sway someone to your point of view. Something is missing. There is another important factor to consider when we are attempting to influence: political savvy.

Political Savvy—A Dirty Word?

Many people have strong and contradictory feelings about being political. In fact, strong negative feelings about politics often present the most significant barrier to making the transition from Hired Hand to Leader.

The roots of the term *political savvy* indicate, however, that our attention should be on others. *Political* comes from the Latin word meaning "the citizens" and *savvy* is from the French verb meaning "to understand." So political savvy is, at its core, **the ability to know the people**.

Political savvy is a crucial leadership skill, and it can be employed in a positive way for positive ends.

Personal Interests vs. Organizational Interests

Below is a model—the Interest Grid—that illustrates what political savvy is and what it is not. The Interest Grid contains four quadrants representing high and low levels of self-interest and organizational interest.

As you read about each quadrant in the model, think about a leader you have known (personally or by reputation) who exemplifies this approach.

THE INTEREST GRID

	low (Organizational Interest)	**high** (Organizational Interest)
high (Self-Interest)	Dysfunctional Politics (Manipulation)	Functional Politics (Savvy)
low (Self-Interest)	Self-Destruction (Career Suicide)	Self-Sacrifice (Martyrdom)

Self-Interest

low   high

Organizational Interest

- **Dysfunctional politics:** People who engage in manipulation (upper left quadrant) promote their own interests at the expense of the organization.

- **Self-destruction:** People who take actions that further neither their own interests, nor those of the organization (lower left quadrant), are engaging in "career suicide." This behavior often signals deep discouragement or burnout.

- **Self-sacrifice:** The lower right quadrant includes people who take actions that further the organization's interests but that ignore their own. They naturally think about what is right for the organization, and they also know that a reputation for putting aside personal agendas builds credibility. However, when overused, this approach can lead to burnout and martyrdom.

- **Political savvy:** In the upper right quadrant are people who make decisions that balance their own interests with those of their organization.

Who Benefits?

Using influence well can actually be a tremendous service to the organization and to the people a leader manages. It can bring the leader's particular unit or department visibility, stature, resources, and a voice in shaping what happens.

On the other hand, lacking or misusing political skills can have very serious consequences to yourself, to your unit, and ultimately even to your ability to achieve emergency management goals in the future.

Building Blocks for Political Savvy

There are three critical building blocks that will help to strengthen your own political skills:

- Alliance Mindset: A mindset focused on alliance.

- Understand Your Allies: The ability to understand your allies.

- Be an Ally: The ability to be an ally to others.

The Alliance Mindset

Viewing others as potential allies is easier said than done. When trying to influence others, you are most likely to see things from your own perspective and remain focused on your own needs. And the more you care about an issue, the more focused on yourself and your position you tend to become.

Yet failing to see others as allies or partners is often a self-fulfilling prophecy. It increases the likelihood that you will act in ways that may actually heighten others' resistance to your ideas.

Therefore, perhaps the most crucial building block of political savvy is your mindset. Leaders who are effective are able to view **and treat** the people around them as partners or potential partners.

The good news is that it is possible to shift from a mindset of seeing people who resist you as adversaries to a mindset of seeing them as potential allies.

The Rules of Alliance

There are four basic rules for interacting with people as your allies:

1. Assume that mutual respect exists.
2. Trust the other person, and be someone whom he or she can trust.
3. Be open; share information.
4. Look for mutual benefits.

Rule 1: Assume that Mutual Respect Exists

Some people will lose your respect by repeatedly taking actions that are boldly self-serving or unethical. But these people are usually the exception, not the rule. More often, you will lose respect for others because of misunderstandings.

Most people involved in emergency management are trying to do the very best that they can in any given situation. By getting better at understanding other people's points of view, you will have a better chance of seeing what motivates them and the context in which they act.

Rule 1 simply challenges you to let yourself be surprised: to start over, suspend your judgment, and assume that respect exists between you. While it may sound idealistic, consider the alternative: when you assume a position of no respect, barriers go up and options shut down.

Rule 2: Trust the Other Person and Be Someone Whom He or She Can Trust

Trusting others means taking a risk and letting your guard down in the hope that something more positive can emerge. Although sometimes it may not be worth the risk, not taking that risk virtually assures that distrust will mount.

In addition to trusting others, being someone whom others can trust is one of the most powerful ways to turn around a troubled relationship. This, too, involves a "calculated leap of faith"—a willingness to take the first step in building or rebuilding a relationship.

It is this kind of risk-taking that is the hallmark of a person working out of the Leader paradigm, someone who breeds commitment and trust by being committed and trustworthy.

Rule 3: Be Open; Share Information

Like the other rules of alliance, this can be a difficult rule to put into practice. Many of us believe that "knowledge is power." Yet power does not necessarily equate with **influence**. You can have a lot of power by hoarding information, but you may not be trusted or respected.

Ask yourself: Would you rather be powerful or effective? The traditionally powerful leader might "know it all," but the person working out of the Leader paradigm who is open and who shares information is more likely to get things done in the long run because of the trust and commitment that he or she builds.

Push past your comfort zone and share more information than you think that you can. See what happens.

Rule 4: Look for Mutual Benefits

You can look for mutual benefits by asking questions and trying to understand the other person's frame of reference. Unfortunately, in typical organizational life, this type of conversation doesn't happen as a matter of course. We often fail to take the time to find out about another person's interests, or we fail to imagine that we might have interests in common.

But these are the prerequisites for finding solutions that are of mutual benefit: taking time to find out about the other person's interests and looking for common interests.

Remember the advice from Unit 2: Inquiry before advocacy. Make sure you take time to listen before you start selling your own ideas. You may find a lot of common ground on which to build.

Looking for mutual benefit is one of the best ways in which to become someone's ally, and to allow them to become yours.

Activity: Applying the Rules of Alliance

Instructions: Think of a current situation in which you and another person are at odds and you want to bring him or her around to your way of thinking. (If no such situation currently exists, think of a past situation.) When you have the situation in mind, answer the following questions.

1. Rule 1 says, "Assume that mutual respect exists." How will you apply this rule? Specifically:

   - How does your past history with this person affect your ability to make this assumption?
   - What will it take for you to assume that mutual respect exists?
   - How can you demonstrate this assumption to the other person?

2. Rule 2 says, "Trust the other person and be someone whom he or she can trust." How can you demonstrate your trust and show that you can be trusted? How might doing this affect your influence in this situation? Are the potential benefits worth the potential risks?

Activity: Applying the Rules of Alliance (Continued)

3. Rule 3 says, "Be open; share information." What are the risks and benefits of sharing information in this situation? What is a first step that you can take in opening up this relationship?

<u>Risks</u>	<u>Benefits</u>

First step:

4. Rule 4 says, "Look for mutual benefits." What potential mutual benefits do you see right now?

What can you do to learn more about other possible mutual benefits in this situation?

Understanding Your Potential Allies

Given the premise that we will be more effective with a mindset that others are our allies, we need to become smarter about who those allies are and what they care about.

Another way of looking at the process of understanding your allies is simply this: You want to make it as easy as possible for them to say "Yes" to you. This requires answers to three questions:

- Who are they?

- What are their concerns, interests, and motivations?

- How does my idea relate to their concerns?

First Question: Who Are Your Allies?

If you are trying to get an idea accepted, your allies might include people:

- Who will or might be affected by your idea.

- Whose cooperation or resources you need to implement your idea.

- Who could benefit and those who could lose.

- Who could block the idea.

- Who could help get it accepted.

Allies include not only obvious supporters, but also those whose support you will need but may not have from the outset.

Case Study 5.2: The Grapevine, Part 2

This case study is a continuation of the case study, "The Grapevine," begun in Unit 4. (If you wish to review that segment, go to page 4.17.) The purpose of this activity is to identify the potential allies in the case study. Read the case study and answer the questions that follow.

Jonas and his team leaders are spending the week with their peers from other departments learning about a new training delivery proposal. During Monday's reception, he approaches a group of managers. During the conversation he learns the following:

- Not all members of senior management are behind the implementation of the new software.

- The problems with the software that his group identified during the pilot still haven't been addressed.

- Everyone is grumbling about why the Information Technology (IT) department didn't fix the problem and why they didn't "kill" the program when they had a chance.

- The Personnel Department is in the process of replacing software that had similar functionality after learning that its vendor will no longer support it. Rick Knowles and Linda Krups, two highly skilled IT people who used to work for Jonas, are now in Personnel, working for Kim Weston.

- Other departments claim that they're not going to use the software. They have concluded that it won't interface with major components of their system and "don't want to mess with it anymore until the Information Technology (IT) people get in and fix it." The interface is critical to accomplishing Gepetta's vision of overhauling deployment procedures and efficiency by the end of the year. If these units don't input the required information at their sites, other employees of the organization won't be able to access it on the system. In that case, Jonas's department will bear the brunt of figuring out how to make it work.

- Many are wondering why IT, which recommended the software initially, didn't address the concerns that were expressed in the pilot and has become neutral on implementation support.

Implementation of the software is a given, either by Jonas or his replacement. His unit provides a critical function for the organization. And although this might not be the perfect software, it's vital to his department's mission.

Case Study 5.2: The Grapevine, Part 2 (Continued)

Identify Jonas's potential allies. Use the following questions to guide your analysis:

1. Outside of Jonas's group, whose time and/or resources does Jonas need to implement this initiative?

2. Who stands to gain from this initiative?

3. Who stands to lose from this initiative?

4. Whose approval does this initiative require?

5. Who does the approver trust and listen to? Who can effectively help Jonas carry his cause?

Case Study 5.2: The Grapevine, Part 2 (Continued)

Possible Answers:

1. Outside of Jonas's group, whose time and/or resources does Jonas need to implement this initiative?

   - The IT Department. (They will need to fix the interface problems.)
   - Other departments' senior managers, managers, and employees. (They will need to implement changes in their units.)

2. Who stands to gain from this initiative?

   - All of the employees who are involved with logistics in any way. (Access to logistical information will be streamlined.)
   - Everyone in the division who is retained (i.e., all but the 15% who are cut).
   - Jonas's department. (The new system will help it discharge its information gathering and reporting functions, which eases everyone's workload.)

3. Who stands to lose from this initiative?

   - The employees who will no longer have jobs.
   - The employees in the other departments who will now have to enter logistics-related information.

4. Whose approval does this initiative require?

   - Senior management
   - The IT department head
   - The department managers

5. Who does the approver trust and listen to? Who can effectively help Jonas carry his cause?

   - Other senior managers
   - Employees who benefit from the system

Second Question: What Are Your Allies' Concerns, Interests, and Motivations?

Knowing who your potential allies are is the first step in understanding them. Your next challenge is to figure out how to influence them. One of the best ways to influence others is to understand their world: their pressures, concerns, and perspectives.

A good example of this, on a broad scale, is the need to understand cultural differences within your community. Cultural differences reflect internal beliefs and thought patterns that can cause people to react differently to the same situation. The same may be true of other special groups—whether defined by age, gender, language differences, special needs, or other characteristics. Their own concerns and interests may color how they interact with you.

To a large extent, the misunderstandings that occur involving people from different cultures or special interest groups have nothing to do with what was said—it's how it was said, what the speaker did while saying it, or even to whom it was said. Clearly, understanding the special needs within your community will enhance the strength of your personal influence.

Whether dealing with an individual or with a group, understanding your allies' interests and motivations is a vital component of political savvy. It is also one of the most under-practiced skills in organizational life, and the place where the process of influence often breaks down. We frequently become so intent on our own idea that we forget to present it in a way that makes it easier for the other person to accept it.

Case Study 5.3: The Grapevine, Part 3

The purpose of this activity is to try to understand potential allies' perspectives in the case study.

1. From the list of potential allies that you identified in the previous activity, write down the names of two people:

   a. **Approver** (The person you think will ultimately approve or disapprove the idea)

   _____

   b. **Enabler** (One other person whose support could help you get the idea accepted. If possible, find someone who probably wouldn't naturally support the idea, but whose support could enhance your chances of getting the idea sold.)

   _____

2. For each of these people: What is this person "on the hook" for in his or her job? What results is he or she primarily accountable for? (e.g., implementing a new program quickly, turning around a difficult department, cutting costs, etc.)

   a. **Approver:**

   b. **Enabler:**

Case Study 5.3: The Grapevine, Part 3 (Continued)

3. For each person: What are their biggest concerns or challenges right now? What impact will those concerns have on Jonas's ability to sell this initiative?

   a. **Approver:**

   b. **Enabler:**

Case Study 5.3: The Grapevine, Part 3 (Continued)

Possible Answers:

1. a. Approver: Kim Weston, head of Personnel.

    b. Enabler: Bob Knowles or Linda Krups, who work for Weston.

2. a. Approver: Implementation of a new system that is similar to the one that Jonas's department has piloted.

    b. Enabler: Establishing greater rapport with the new boss and supporting the new system.

3. a. Approver: A system is needed to replace the one that is being phased out. Ms. Weston is facing additional costs and/or time pressures to complete the system change.

    b. Enabler: Supporting Ms. Weston's efforts will place additional demands on his or her time. He or she might be asked to do the research.

However, you may not have known as much as you needed to about your potential allies. For example, were you sure who your approvers and enablers would be? Did you feel confident in knowing the concerns and perspectives of the people you identified?

This type of knowledge might change your thinking about how best to position your idea. And not knowing enough (identifying blind spots) should lead you to finding out more so that you can use personal influence to help achieve your objectives.

The point is, people will support your ideas when they can see the merits from their own points of view. Even though your idea is a great one to you, if it works against the interests of the people whose support you need, it will be unlikely to gain acceptance.

Understanding what your potential allies care about is a key to positive influence. It helps you present your ideas in a way that benefits all concerned.

Remember—**the ability to take action that serves both you and the organization is the hallmark of political savvy**.

Third Question: How Does My Idea Relate to Their Concern?

First, you identified your potential allies in relation to your situation. Next, you focused on two of them—the approver and an enabler—and tried to understand more about what they care about. The third step is to relate your ideas to those of your allies and to position your idea in a way that makes it easy for these allies to say "Yes."

To complete this step, you need to answer two sets of questions:

- **In what ways could my initiative support their priorities? Are there ways in which my initiative might work against that person's objectives?**

  In the case study, Jonas might conclude that the system could be modified to meet the needs of Kim Weston (i.e., of Personnel). His department has already done the research and tested its specifications, which would save them time and money. A deal is already in place with the vendor to support needed modifications. Jonas could also offer to partner with Personnel to get IT aboard. On the other hand, the proposal could work against them if the package doesn't meet their needs.

  Regarding the enablers, Jonas might conclude that if Bob and Linda are assigned to do the research, Logistics could share their research with them or offer to put them in touch with the vendor. If they have to work with IT, he could offer to join them in the endeavor.

- **How could I modify either my idea or my presentation of it so that it would be more attractive to these people?**

  Jonas's answer might be that Logistics could agree to have their system modified to meet Personnel's needs as well, and they could offer to work with Bob and Linda to gather the design specifications.

The key point is this: Viewing people as allies opens up new possibilities of interacting with them in more positive, effective, and savvy ways.

Being an Ally to Others

We have talked about the importance of having an alliance mindset and of understanding your allies. The third building block for political savvy is to be an ally.

Principle of Reciprocity

Being an ally means invoking the principle of reciprocity:

> **As we do things for others in organizations,
> they become more likely to help us in return.**

It is important to realize that this is NOT a "scratch my back and I'll scratch your back" approach. It is also not a tit-for-tat trade where, to get a specific idea through, you promise something in return.

Rather, it means being a friend to others in the organization, because by helping others you will also be helping the organization and helping yourself.

Keep thinking of the metaphor of friendship: You are more willing to support a friend who has been there for you than to support someone who has never shown any particular kindness in the past. The same holds true for organizations. Being an ally means creating a web of good will in which others will be, in turn, more inclined to help you at a time when you need it.

> **Caution:** It will be too late to start being an ally at the point when you need something from someone else. People see right through this as manipulation. Being an ally means taking a day-in and day-out stance of helpfulness, whether you need something today—or ever—from that person.

Principle of Reciprocity (Continued)

On the other hand, this principle of reciprocity could sound like a plea just to be a nice person. And while that's true, the politically astute people have discovered that treating others well also turns out to be smart business.

These words best sum up the idea of being an ally:

Become the change you wish to see in the world.

–Mahatma Ghandi

Activity: Your Personal Influence and Political Savvy

Situational Influence

1. **Identify a situation.** Think about something that you would like to make happen in your professional situation (e.g., getting an idea adopted, instituting a change, implementing a program or initiative, forging an alliance with another organization or jurisdiction, or solving a problem).

2. **Who are your potential allies in this situation?** Identify:

   - Who might be affected by your idea (those who could benefit, those who could lose, and others who would be affected):

   - Whose cooperation and/or resources you need:

   - Who could block the idea:

   - Who could help get it accepted:

Activity: Your Personal Influence and Political Savvy (Continued)

3. **What are your allies' concerns, interests, and motivations?**
   Select one person you identified in each of the ally categories. Describe what you can about their perspective. If you don't know, how can you find out more?

   - The affected:

   - The needed:

   - The blockers:

   - The enablers:

Activity: Your Personal Influence and Political Savvy (Continued)

4. Select the two potentially strongest allies from those you identified earlier, then answer the following questions about each.

	Ally #1: _____	Ally #2: _____
How could your idea support their priorities?		
How could your idea work against them?		
How could you modify your plan or your presentation of it to make it more attractive to them?		

Activity: Your Personal Influence and Political Savvy (Continued)

Positional Influence

1. In your emergency management role, what groups must you influence if you are to be successful? (Think generally—not just about the situation that you have been analyzing.)

2. For each group identified above, list the factors that will affect how the group can be influenced.

Activity: Your Personal Influence and Political Savvy (Continued)

3. Identify three strategies for becoming a better ally, over time, to these groups. Your strategies must meet the following criteria:

    - **Usefulness:** They must be actions that would be genuinely useful to others.
    - **Integrity:** They must be actions that are honestly worth doing, whether they ever "buy" you anything in return.

Strategy #1:

Strategy #2:

Strategy #3:

Developing a "Win-Win" Solution

Have you ever watched a cat negotiate with a mouse? The cat may allow the mouse some latitude in its actions, but always within the boundaries determined by the cat. Once in a while, the mouse will find a crack in the porch steps through which it escapes to achieve its goals.

In negotiations, do you feel like the cat or the mouse? Is there another way to negotiate?

There are several points to remember when striving for a "win-win" solution:

- Define the conflict as a mutual problem. Be certain that the identification of the conflict includes:

  - A clear definition or statement of the issue.
  - All of the information that is needed to solve the issue.
  - Internal and external factors that affect the issue.
  - A blame-free environment for describing the issue.

  When people involved can see the situation objectively, they can share in the realization that everyone "owns" the problem and the solution.

- Apply active listening skills to the communication process. Ask yourself: What elements of the issues will active listening find that are important in reaching a "win-win" solution? These elements should include:

  - The emotions behind the issue.
  - External pressure factors.

- Focus on the interests, rather than on positions. Sometimes, people enter negotiations with <u>position</u> statements rather than with <u>interest</u> statements.

Summary and Transition

Unit 5 focused on the role of leader as a politically savvy influencer and the skills for effectively influencing others. Unit 6 discusses strategies for fostering a leadership environment.

For More Information

Books:

- *Political Savvy: Systematic Approaches to Leadership Behind the Scenes.* DeLuca, Joel R. LRP Publications, 1999.

- *Influence: Science and Practice.* Cialdini, Robert B. New York: Allyn & Bacon, 2000.

Knowledge Check

Carefully read each question and all of the possible answers before selecting the most appropriate response for each test item. Circle the letter corresponding to the answer that you have chosen. Complete all of the questions without looking at the course material.

1. Two people have the following conversation:
   Person A: "I think we could use a training session to orient managers to the new emergency management procedures."
   Person B: "You're right. The new procedures are complicated. What you've said makes me think that we should train employees at all levels, not just managers."

   This is an example of:

   a. Constructive disagreement
   b. Position influence
   c. Domineering influence
   d. Building on ideas

2. Political savvy refers to:

   a. Promoting one's own interests over all others.
   b. Sacrificing one's own interests for those of the organization.
   c. Adhering to the premise that "knowledge is power."
   d. The ability to balance one's own interests with those of the organization.

3. The ability to understand one's allies and to be an ally to others are two building blocks for political savvy. The third is:

   a. The ability to silence your detractors.
   b. The ability to view and treat people as allies.
   c. Recognizing those who resist you as adversaries.
   d. Being willing to abandon your interests for the greater good.

4. Assuming that you and another person share mutual respect can eliminate barriers and open up options.

   a. True
   b. False

5. People who oppose you in the beginning can be potentially strong allies.

   a. True
   b. False

Knowledge Check (Continued)

6. After you understand a potential ally's interests and motivations, you should:

    a. Try to determine how your idea relates to their concerns.
    b. Use that knowledge to get the upper hand.
    c. Convince them to abandon their interests.
    d. Give up on them as allies if their motivations differ from yours.

7. The underlying principle of being an ally to others is:

    a. Make sure that you're a member of the inner circle of power.
    b. Tit-for-tat (influence lies in trading favors).
    c. Treating others well helps them, you, and the organization.
    d. Wait until you need them, then be their best friend.

Knowledge Check (Continued)
1. d
2. d
3. b
4. a
5. a
6. a
7. c

Unit 6: Fostering a Leadership Environment

Introduction

In previous units, we have explored attributes that a leader in emergency management needs to have: self-knowledge, ability to facilitate change, the capacity to build and rebuild trust, and personal influence and political savvy. Another hallmark of effective leaders is the ability to create an environment that develops the future generation of leaders and fosters leadership qualities at every level, in every employee. In fact, this is one of the most significant legacies that you can leave the organization: leaders who are equipped to lead in whatever disasters the future will bring. In this unit, we will look at strategies for fostering a leadership environment.

Unit 6 Objectives

After completing this unit, you should be able to:

- Describe the leader's role in developing leadership qualities in others.

- Develop strategies for creating a positive work environment.

Fostering Leaders in Emergency Management

The critical difference in successful emergency response organizations is that the successful organization maximizes the use of the "intellectual capital" found in the organization's members. Organizations that are unable or unwilling to make use of the intellectual capital will be ineffective in an emergency.

Exemplary emergency response systems rely on the capabilities of all the personnel involved, not just those of a few in leadership positions. To create a successful emergency response system, leaders must take advantage of the vast knowledge and know-how of all those involved in making a response successful—whether internal or external to the emergency management agency. The 1991 book, *Leadership Secrets of Atilla the Hun* by Wes Roberts is a very interesting series of lessons about a leader who made the most of his people.

Strategies for Fostering Leadership

In previous units, you learned about several ways you can foster leadership. Among them were:

- Developing Leader qualities that emphasize a view of the organization as a moral system, drawing credibility and power from behavioral integrity and core values, and being motivated by realization of the vision.

- Expanding your self-knowledge and making more of your hidden self visible to others.

- Encouraging authentic feedback for self-improvement.

- Using the Ladder of Inference to create an environment of leadership.

- Nurturing an environment of shared learning by balancing inquiry and advocacy.

- Facilitating acceptance of change within the organization.

- Building and maintaining a climate of trust.

- Using personal influence and political savvy to help achieve the vision and goals of the organization.

Strategies for Developing Leaders

The strategies just mentioned comprise a comprehensive approach you can use, not only to strengthen your own leadership skills, but also to create an environment in which new leaders can grow. In addition to these general approaches, there are some specific strategies that effective leaders use to encourage the developing leaders in their organization.

Some of these strategies are briefly described below. Each one of them constitutes a broad topic that could merit an entire course of its own. You may wish to seek additional information on some of these topics to expand your leadership skills further.

Building a Shared Vision

Effective leaders create a shared vision of great performance—a clear picture of the future of the organization, based on tomorrow's needs. The vision makes the goal and the journey clear: where we are going, how we will know when we get there, and how we'll know that we're making progress. Effective leaders see the total system, understand it, and help others to understand it.   And they help to build the power within the organization to achieve the vision.

Effective leaders encourage employees at all levels to expand, deepen, and personalize the organizational vision by identifying how, in their own roles, they can make a significant contribution to achieving the organizational vision.

Empowerment

An effective leader empowers employees by developing a shared vision, removing obstacles to great performance, developing ownership of the vision among the employees, and stimulating self-directed actions. The leader must be sure that the performers are responsible and accountable for great performance. People who are given a real voice are much more likely to "buy in" to the vision and the organizational goals and to make it their mission to help achieve those goals.

Team Building

Effective leaders build a team environment in which members pool their resources and rely on each other to achieve common goals. As people combine their energies, the cooperative action of the group creates a greater result than the individuals could accomplish working separately.   A leader promotes a team environment by:

- Establishing an environment of trust.

- Setting up systems and structures to require teamwork.

- Encouraging team communication to build team identity.

- Fostering the evolution of natural leadership abilities in group members.

- Establishing team goals and team rewards (i.e., reward team effort).

- Celebrating group achievements, even those which are minor.

Coaching

A leader who manages through coaching convinces people of their own ability to do the job. They have faith that, with the proper training and support, people will excel. Coaching involves providing training, support, and constructive feedback as an employee carries out responsibilities. The leader gives ongoing encouragement and praise for successes and helps the person build confidence in his or her own abilities.

An effective format for coaching includes these steps:

- Set the stage. Give full attention, be clear, assume a "shared learning" mindset, encourage dialogue, listen actively, and foster mutual respect.

- Define the problem, goal, or issue. Be specific and be clear about your assumptions.

- Foster a growth atmosphere by reinforcing positive behavior, making clear that you are there to help, and encouraging the open exchange of ideas.

- Provide opportunities for collaboration and problemsolving on alternatives. Apply the principles of balanced inquiry and advocacy, constructive disagreement, and idea-building in exploring alternatives. Give constructive feedback to improve performance.

- Agree on an action plan and set a follow-up date, then keep the door open.

Delegation

Do what you do best, and give away the rest to someone else. An effective leader delegates broad responsibilities to team members and expects them to handle the details. Delegating responsibilities to capable personnel has many advantages. It distributes the workload, results in higher efficiency and increased motivation, and develops the skills of the workforce. People learn more by doing than by any other means. Delegation provides opportunities for people to develop leadership skills.

Effective delegation involves:

- Identifying an appropriate person for the task.

- Preparing the person by clearly stating desired outcomes while encouraging risk-taking and innovation.

- Ensuring that the person has the necessary authority to do the job properly.

- Holding the person accountable for agreed-upon outcomes.

- Maintaining enough contact for support and monitoring of progress without "hovering."

- Acknowledging success and giving credit where it is due.

Mentoring

Effective leaders use mentoring to foster leadership skills within the organization. Mentoring happens when an experienced person provides guidance and support in a variety of ways to a developing employee, introducing that person to the workings of the organization and assisting with professional development. A mentor must be willing to share his or her expertise and not be threatened by the concept of the person's success within the organization.

Activity: Fostering Leadership in Your Environment

As a leader, you must draw on the self-knowledge we discussed earlier and consider the changes that you will need to make in your own behavior to maximize the contribution of every person in your organization to prevention, preparedness, response, recovery, and mitigation.

To begin, consider your emergency planning process—who is involved (internally and externally) and how they work together. Use the space below to make notes if you wish.

When you have outlined the key points of your process, you will analyze the current working relationships and develop a strategy for maximizing each person's contribution to the system. Use the questions on the following pages to guide your analysis.

Activity: Fostering Leadership in Your Environment (Continued)

1. What is your role as a leader in creating the current culture?

2. How effectively does the system function within the current culture?

3. What can you do to improve the culture? (What structures can you put in place?)

Activity: Fostering Leadership in Your Environment (Continued)

4. What skills do you need to change the culture in a positive direction?

5. What obstacles will get in the way? How will you overcome them? What do you need to influence the necessary changes?

Activity: Fostering Leadership in Your Environment (Continued)

6. When these changes occur, in what ways will they impact response operations?

7. In what ways will they impact the public?

___

Summary and Transition

In Unit 6, you learned strategies for fostering an environment that supports your own leadership development and encourages leadership throughout the organization. You also developed a strategy for improving the leadership environment in your emergency management system.

Before you proceed to the summary unit for this course, take a few minutes to review your understanding of strategies for fostering a leadership environment by completing the Knowledge Check on the next page.

For More Information

Books:

- *Flight of the Buffalo: Soaring to Excellence, Learning to Let Employees Lead.* Belasco, James A. and Stayer, Ralph C. New York: Warner Books, 1994.

- *The 21 Indispensable Qualities of a Leader: Becoming the Person Others Will Want to Follow.* Maxwell, John C. Thomas Nelson Pub., 1999.

- *The 3 Keys to Empowerment: Release the Power Within People for Astonishing Results.* Blanchard, Ken; Carlos, John C.; and Randolph, Alan. Berrett-Koehler Publishers Inc., 1999.

- *Gung Ho! Turn on the People in Any Organization.* Blanchard, Kenneth H., and Bowles, Sheldon. William Morrow & Co., 1997.

Knowledge Check

Carefully read each question and all of the possible answers before selecting the most appropriate response for each test item. Circle the letter corresponding to the answer that you have chosen. Complete all of the questions without looking at the course material.

1. In a leadership environment:

   a. Leadership and responsibility are shared by all.
   b. The manager is the expert and final authority, and controls the outcomes.
   c. No one leads because everything is done in teams.
   d. Everyone has his or her own agenda.

2. Organizations that depend on members' intellectual capital at all levels:

   a. Will find themselves without recognized leaders.
   b. Run the risk of dissolving into chaos.
   c. Are only as strong as the weakest link.
   d. Have a greater pool of resources from which to draw.

3. Emergency management leaders should confine their leadership development efforts to personnel within the emergency management agency and let the rest of the response system develop its own strategies.

   a. True
   b. False

4. A climate of trust:

   a. Is unrelated to the leadership environment.
   b. Undermines the leadership environment.
   c. Is an important aspect of a leadership environment.
   d. Serves as a useful alternative to a leadership environment.

5. A leader who delegates:

   a. Is helping to build leadership skills.
   b. Can avoid taking responsibility for outcomes.
   c. Should give responsibility but not authority.
   d. Should resist the temptation to follow up on progress.

Knowledge Check (Continued)

1. a
2. d
3. b
4. c
5. a

Unit 7: Course Summary

Introduction

This unit will briefly summarize the learning from the Leadership and Influence course. When you finish with this unit, be sure to take the final exam that is available for download from the Emergency Management Institute's Independent Study Web site: http://training.fema.gov/IS/

Leadership and Influence in Emergency Management

A leader is one who sets direction and influences people to follow that direction. Leadership is critically important in emergency management, and lack of it can result in loss of public trust, loss of property, and loss of life. The need for leadership applies across all of the phases of emergency management: prevention, preparedness, response, recovery, and mitigation.

Leadership from Within

Part of being an effective leader is the ability to create an environment that encourages self-discovery and the testing of assumptions that may impede growth, change, and the development of a shared vision. Self-knowledge helps leaders develop their strengths as leaders.

Leadership Paradigms

There are three paradigms that relate to the development of leadership skills:

- The Hired Hand

- The Broker

- The Leader

These paradigms provide different ways of looking at the world. They are not mutually exclusive, and managers use all of them in one situation or another. But an effective leader has more of the attributes of the Leader Paradigm.

Leadership Paradigms (Continued)

Leaders:

- View the organization as a moral system.

- Derive credibility and power from behavioral integrity and core values.

- Are motivated to a higher purpose.

- Approach challenges with a variety of perspectives and approaches.

- Give careful thought to the meaning of their actions.

- Are focused and committed to a vision of the common good.

Increasing Self-Knowledge

Leaders need to develop self-knowledge to grow. Part of this knowledge is being aware of the paradigms in which they operate and being willing to set aside comfortable behaviors to grow. It is also important to open up to others so as to build effective relationships.

Three methods for increasing self-knowledge are:

- Self-assessment.

- Self-reflection.

- Soliciting authentic feedback.

Another area in which leaders need to expand their self-knowledge is understanding how they think and what assumptions, biases, and beliefs they bring to their relationships. The "Ladder of Inference" is a mental model that describes how we process our experiences and merge them with our beliefs and assumptions.

Balancing Inquiry and Advocacy

Leaders need to balance inquiry (using interaction with other people to learn, exchange ideas, and understand their perspectives) and advocacy (evaluating ideas, promoting one's own idea, and working toward consensus).

Facilitating Change

Being able to respond quickly and effectively to change is crucial for emergency response systems. Being able to facilitate change in the organization is a hallmark of an effective leader.

Change Model

An effective change process includes the following stages:

- **Defining and Promoting the Change:** The leader must define what the change is, why it is necessary, what the change means to individuals and the organization, and why the change needs to happen now.

- **Planning and Implementing the Change:** It is vital to understand the change process, how to effectively manage it, and how to address any problems that could arise.

- **Maintaining the Change:** The leader must continually engaging those whose support of the process is critical; listen to staff concerns and respond to staff needs; and provide staff with what they need, both physically and mentally, to support the change.

- **Engaging the People in the Change:** Maintaining change is largely about maintaining relationships with people during the change process, including asking for feedback during the process, accepting a wide range of responses to the change, and effectively and sincerely responding to the staff feedback and requests

Communicating Change

To facilitate change in an organization successfully, the leader must be able to communicate effectively the "3 W's and 1 H".

- **Why?** What is the purpose of the change?

- **What?** What is the vision of the organization and the staff after the change?

- **How?** What is the plan for accomplishing this change?

- **Who?** What is everyone's role in the process?

Four rules for communicating change are:

- **Communicate** first through actions, then words.

- **Recognize** that perceptions will become distorted.

- **Remember** the "rule of six" (tell people six times in six ways).

- **Anticipate** and **allow** for strong emotions.

Building and Rebuilding Trust

A leader can't effectively facilitate change without mutual trust, but it is very difficult to build trust in a changing environment or to rebuild trust after it is lost. Therefore, one of the most critical aspects of the leader's job is to build an environment of trust. Trust is the very core of leadership, and trust must be earned.

Trust is a relationship based on mutual confidence that both parties will:

- Do what they say.

- Communicate honestly.

- Respect one another's knowledge, skills, and abilities.

- Maintain confidentiality.

- Keep their interactions unguarded.

Building Trust

Building and nurturing trust in the workplace requires leaders who:

- Honestly describe any situation they are in, including discussing any loss of trust that has occurred.
- Respect others and relationships with them during tough times as well as when things are smooth sailing.
- Nurture understanding and empathy with themselves and with others.
- Desire to build and maintain a cooperative organizational culture.

A trusting relationship is a two-way street. An effective leader is both worthy of trust and able to trust others. A leader can build people's faith in his or her trustworthiness through:

- Predictable behavior.

- Clear communication.

- Keeping promises.

- Being forthright.

Although the capacity for trusting others is influenced by history, the situation, the inherent risk, and other factors, a leader can expand the capacity for trust by giving people the benefit of the doubt and by looking for opportunities to stretch beyond the comfort zone to demonstrate trust.

Rebuilding Trust

Building trust is a slow process, and trust can be destroyed by a single event. When trust breaks down, a leader can use the following steps to begin to rebuild trust:

1. Accept responsibility.
2. Admit the mistake.
3. Apologize.
4. Act to deal with the consequences.
5. Make amends.
6. Attend to people's reactions and concerns.

Personal Influence and Political Savvy

In addition to building trust and facilitating change, an effective leader must be able to exert personal influence to achieve goals. An emergency management professional must be able to exercise influence in multiple directions:

- Upward (with those of higher rank).

- Laterally (with peers in the same organization or the response system).

- Downward (with subordinates).

- Outward (with people outside the organization, including the media, the public, the business community, and others).

Types of Influence

There are three types of influence:

- Position influence.

- Domineering influence.

- Interpersonal influence.

Although leaders may use all three types of influence in different situations, it is interpersonal influence that lays a foundation for trust, support, and collaboration.

Effective interpersonal influence involves three elements: I, You, and We. Together, they add up to, "I am a trustworthy ally, you are a valuable resource, and we can accomplish this together."

Negotiating Agreement

An effective leader needs to be able to react appropriately to another person's point of view to foster a win/win outcome. Negotiating agreement involves three skills:

- **Agreeing:** Stating what you like about the other person's idea and why you like it.

- **Constructive disagreement:** Framing disagreement with an idea in a way that preserves the person's self-esteem. This involves identifying the value of the idea, explaining your reservations, and discussing alternatives.

- **Building on ideas:** Acknowledging the connection and adding value.

Political Savvy

There are times when, in addition to personal influence, the leader needs political savvy, which is, literally, the ability to know people. Political savvy can be used in a positive way, for positive ends.

Political savvy represents a balance between self-interest and organizational interest. Using influence well can benefit not only the manager, but the organization as a whole and the people the manager leads.

Three building blocks for political savvy are:

- An alliance mindset.

- The ability to understand one's allies.

- The ability to be an ally to others.

Rules of Alliance

An alliance mindset involves viewing others as potential allies. There are four rules for interacting with people as allies:

- Assume that mutual respect exists.

- Trust the other person, and be someone whom he or she can trust.

- Be open; share information.

- Look for mutual benefits.

Understanding One's Allies

An effective leader is smart about who his or her allies are and what they care about. To develop this understanding, the leader needs to ask:

- **Who are my allies?** (They may include those who may be affected, whose cooperation is needed, who could present obstacles, or who could help build support.)

- **What are their concerns, interests, and motivations?** ("Walking a mile in the other person's shoes" will help you know how to influence them.)

- **How does my idea relate to their concerns?** (You need to understand how your idea may help or hurt them, and how you could adjust your thinking to better accommodate their needs.)

Being an Ally to Others

Being an ally means invoking the principle of reciprocity: As we do things for others in the organization, they become more likely to help us in return. In other words, build good will every day and it will be there when you need it.

Fostering a Leadership Environment

One of the most significant legacies that you can leave an organization is to have created a new generation of leaders. Being able to create an environment that promotes the development of new leaders, and at the same time nurtures your own leadership skills, is the hallmark of a truly effective leader.

All of the strategies just reviewed (developing self-knowledge, balancing inquiry and advocacy, building trust, and so on) contribute to a leadership environment. In addition, a leader can encourage leadership development in others through such activities as:

- Building a shared vision.

- Empowering others.

- Creating a team environment.

- Coaching.

- Delegating.

- Mentoring.

Next Steps

You have now completed IS-240 and should be ready to take the final exam.

Complete the final exam in the back of the book by marking the correct responses.

To submit the final exam online:

1. Go to http://training.fema.gov/IS/
2. Click on the Courses link.
3. Click on the title for this course.
4. Scroll down the course description page to locate the final exam link.
5. After you have selected the final exam link and the online answer sheet is open, transfer your answers, and complete the personal identification data requested.

To submit the final exam by mail using the standard answer sheet, follow the instructions printed on the form.

Good luck!

Appendix A: Job Aids

Job Aid 2.1: Self-Reflection Techniques

Journal Writing

Journal writing is one technique for self-reflection. Approached in the right way, it can be a process of *discovery* rather than mere **reporting**. Productive journal writing takes very little time and can be of great benefit. It can be a powerful tool for reflection, self-discovery, problem solving, learning, and integration. Here's how it works:

1. Think about a situation at work with which you are currently struggling or feeling unsettled. (This technique is also good for situations in your personal life.)

2. Write down a set of questions you want to reflect on concerning the situation. Put each question on a separate page, to allow lots of room to write. For starters, try these questions:

   a. What about this situation is uncomfortable or difficult for me?
   b. What did I learn about myself and/or the situation?
   c. What are all of the possible steps I can think of to take, based on what I've just learned?

   As you become familiar with this technique, you can vary the questions to accommodate your own needs for personal growth.

3. Decide on a time limit (for example, 3 minutes per question). If possible, set a timer so you don't have to watch the time.

4. Begin writing. Write about the first question *continuously* for the allotted time. Write whatever comes to your mind. Don't worry about grammar or punctuation. Just *do not stop writing* until the time is up.

5. Respond in the same manner, writing continuously, to each question.

Try this technique every day for a week before you decide whether this approach is a good one for you.

Job Aid 2.1: Self-Reflection Techniques (Continued)

Thinking Out Loud

Thinking out loud is another self-reflection technique. It is quite simple and can be done with a partner or alone, using a tape recorder. These are the ground rules:

1. The partner has only one role: to listen. He or she should not provide suggestions, advice, or insert him- or herself at all in the speaker's process.

2. Select a situation with which you are currently struggling or feeling unsettled, which you will talk about.

3. You may wish to set up a timeframe in advance (e.g., 1 minute to set the context and 4 minutes to speak).

4. Talk.

5. Afterwards, review what you said: Either discuss it with your partner or replay your tape. Many people find that having a "sounding board"—someone to listen without trying to solve their problem—unleashes their creative problem-solving abilities.

Job Aid 3.1: Change Process Questions

The following questions relate to each of the stages of the change process. When applying the process to a change situation that you face, you can use these questions to analyze the situation and develop strategies for effecting change.

Defining and Promoting the Change

- What must happen for this change to be successful? How should this be communicated to employees or other stakeholders?
- What are the opportunities associated with the change? How can the fear be taken out of the change?
- How can you demonstrate continuous support for and sponsorship of this change initiative?
- In what specific ways can you be a catalyst rather than a controller of the change?
- What challenges might you encounter in balancing the needs of the organization and those of individuals? How can you manage these challenges?
- How can you "walk the talk" during this change initiative? What pitfalls will you need to avoid?
- What is the rationale for this change? That is, what are we trying to accomplish with the change? How should this be communicated to employees or other stakeholders?
- How can the change initiative be linked to the organization's or the community's strategy, mission, and environment?
- What mechanisms can be used to keep lines of communication with employees and/or stakeholders open and to inform them of progress being made?

Planning and Implementing the Change

- What is the vision for this change—i.e., what would you like to see happen as a result of this change? What do you see as the benefits of the change?
- What are the major components of a plan for this change?
- How can you keep employees and/or stakeholders involved in the process?
- What potential problems and opportunities are associated with this change?
- What existing systems might need to be modified to reinforce needed changes?
- What mechanisms should be put in place for monitoring and evaluating the implementation of the change?
- What potential resistance points might you encounter? How can you manage this resistance?
- How might production be impacted and how can you manage this?
- What resources will be needed to implement this change successfully? How can you secure these resources?
- What interim systems might you need to implement? How should they be implemented?

Job Aid 3.1: Change Process Questions (Continued)

Maintaining the Change

- What formal and informal mechanisms can you use to communicate the change?
- How can you sustain energy and commitment to this change over time?
- Whose support will be critical to the successful implementation of this change? How will you gain their support?
- What might employees and/or stakeholders need to accept and support this change?
- What small successes can you celebrate? How?

Engaging the People in the Change

- What reactions to this change initiative do you anticipate from employees and/or stakeholders?
- What pitfalls should you avoid when responding to these reactions?
- What mechanisms can you use to solicit employee and/or stakeholder concerns? How can you demonstrate that you are listening to their concerns about the change?
- In what ways can you monitor their comments and feedback?